Opening up Proverbs

JIM NEWHEISER

Prov. 3:5-6

DayOne

Proverbs packs its punches—and so does Jim Newheiser's survey of it! Living in a fallen world is full of dangers for Christians as well as opportunities for serving God and one's neighbour in love. Newheiser shows repeatedly and incisively how the best life consists in avoiding the former (folly) and engaging in the latter (wisdom) out of 'the fear of the LORD' that is love to Christ.

Hywel R. Jones
Professor of Practical Theology,
Westminster Seminary, California

In an age of open-mindedness and an abysmal lack of discernment in the church, scores of Christians grope for easy and instant solutions to life's problems. Sadly, they turn away from the wise counsel of God's Word to embrace teachings that can only lead to serious error. But like few other books that have seen print of late, Jim Newheiser's commentary on the book of Proverbs comes as a refreshing breeze. This book is a practical, encouraging, and insightful guide to godly living. Jim carefully weaves the wise sayings of this beloved and ancient book into a cohesive unit with clarity, balance, and a deep commitment to God's glory, while unlocking helpful principles that address problems in marriage, parenting, communication, work, wealth, and other aspects in life where we are routinely challenged. This highly readable book is a wholesome prescription for today's Christian.

Bob Amigo
Pastor of Higher Rock Christian Church,
Quezon City (Manila), Philippines

The book of Proverbs has long been a favourite of mine. During our fifty-plus years of marriage, my wife and I have read through and discussed the contents of the book many times. We have done the same with each of our children, and I remember the benefit I received from being part of a men's group that worked its way through the book over a period of more than a year. And, being a biblical counsellor, I have often used many portions of the book in counselling or given it to counsellees as a homework assignment. In my studies of Proverbs, Bruce Waltke's and Charles Bridges' commentaries on the book have proved very helpful. Now, Jim Newheiser builds on these works and does a marvellous job of arranging and explaining the contents of the book in a very practical way. As I read through Newheiser's comments, I found myself being

challenged and receiving fresh insights for my own personal life and for my ministry to others. Thank you, Jim, for bringing the contents of this divinely inspired book (Proverbs) to us in such a refreshing and relevant way. I commend it without reservation.

Dr Wayne Mack
(M.Div., Philadelphia Theological Seminary; D.Min., Westminster Theological Seminary),
Director of Strengthening Ministries International, Professor of Biblical Counselling at The Master's College, Los Angeles and Little Rock, Arkansas, and a founding member of the National Association of Nouthetic Counselors (USA)

First printed 2008

ISBN 978–1–84625–110–8

British Library Cataloguing in Publication Data available

Published by Day One Publications
Ryelands Road, Leominster, England, HR6 8NZ
Telephone 01568 613 740 FAX 01568 611 473

email—sales@dayone.co.uk
web site—www.dayone.co.uk
North American—e-mail-sales@dayonebookstore.com
North American web site—www.dayonebookstore.com

Printed in Canada

Contents

With gratitude to Dr Bruce Waltke, whose messages on Proverbs, given at Believers Chapel, Dallas, Texas, in the 1970s, have been the voice of wisdom to me as I have sought to understand this great book. The wisdom I gained from him permeates this volume.

With deepest appreciation to God for my wife, who is a true woman of virtue who has done me good and not evil all the days of her life (Prov. 31:11–12, 28–31), and for my mother, who showed me the kind of wife I should find (Prov. 31:1–10).

With thanks to my faithful proofreaders Pat, Cindi, Kayla, James and Jenny.

List of Bible abbreviations

THE OLD TESTAMENT

Gen.	Genesis
Exod.	Exodus
Lev.	Leviticus
Num.	Numbers
Deut.	Deuteronomy
Josh.	Joshua
Judg.	Judges
Ruth	Ruth
1 Sam.	1 Samuel
2 Sam.	2 Samuel
1 Kings	1 Kings
2 Kings	2 Kings
1 Chr.	1 Chronicles
2 Chr.	2 Chronicles
Ezra	Ezra
Neh.	Nehemiah
Esth.	Esther
Job	Job
Ps.	Psalms
Prov.	Proverbs
Eccles.	Ecclesiastes
S. of. S.	Song of Solomon
Isa.	Isaiah
Jer.	Jeremiah
Lam.	Lamentations
Ezek.	Ezekiel
Dan.	Daniel
Hosea	Hosea
Joel	Joel
Amos	Amos
Obad.	Obadiah
Jonah	Jonah
Micah	Micah
Nahum	Nahum
Hab.	Habakkuk
Zeph.	Zephaniah
Hag.	Haggai
Zech.	Zechariah
Mal.	Malachi

THE NEW TESTAMENT

Matt.	Matthew
Mark	Mark
Luke	Luke
John	John
Acts	Acts
Rom.	Romans
1 Cor.	1 Corinthians
2 Cor.	2 Corinthians
Gal.	Galatians
Eph.	Ephesians
Phil.	Philippians
Col.	Colossians
1 Thes.	1 Thessalonians
2 Thes.	2 Thessalonians
1 Tim.	1 Timothy
2 Tim.	2 Timothy
Titus	Titus
Philem.	Philemon
Heb.	Hebrews
James	James
1 Peter	1 Peter
2 Peter	2 Peter
1 John	1 John
2 John	2 John
3 John	3 John
Jude	Jude
Rev.	Revelation

Introduction

Study Proverbs for success

My family often plays a game called 'Careers', the object of which is to be the first to accumulate a certain combination of money, fame, and happiness. A player goes around the board making choices that lead to the acquisition or loss of cash, stars (representing fame), and hearts (representing happiness). The first player to achieve his or her goals wins. These elements of material wealth, celebrity, and pleasure form the definition of success for many in the West. Such values have also infiltrated the church as many professing Christians have adopted worldly measures of accomplishment and many churches pander to these bankrupt values.

The Bible sets forth an entirely different measure of success. Success is found in living wisely in the fear of the LORD. To live wisely is to live beautifully—that is, to live a life that counts.

The book of Proverbs reveals how you can have success in every aspect of your life. Do you want to have a joyous and fruitful marriage? Do you want to enjoy success in raising your children? Do you want to prosper in your career? Do you want to have fulfilling relationships with others? Do you want to learn how to speak with wisdom and grace? Study the Proverbs and learn to live by them.

The uniqueness of biblical proverbs

The collecting of proverbs is not unique to the Bible. We have certain proverbs in English—such as 'a stitch in time saves nine' or 'you can lead a horse to water, but you can't make him drink'—that express commonly accepted wisdom. Solomon was not the only man in the ancient world who took interest in wise sayings. Others, including the Egyptians and Babylonians, had wise men who spoke and collected proverbs. It is not surprising that these proverbs have similarities with those in the Bible. Through common grace, even unbelievers recognize many aspects of God's moral order. It may even be that Solomon incorporated some of the sayings of other cultures into the biblical book of Proverbs (1 Kings 4:30–34).

Through common grace, even unbelievers recognize many aspects of God's moral order.

The biblical proverbs are unique, however, because they are grounded in covenant relation with the LORD God: 'The fear of the LORD is the beginning of knowledge' (1:7*a*). Solomon doesn't merely offer clever sayings that provide useful advice on how to enjoy worldly success; rather, he teaches that true wisdom and success are rooted in having a right relationship with God, who is the source of all wisdom. Worldly wisdom, like other counterfeits, may appear at first to be similar to the genuine article, but closer examination reveals essential differences. 'The wisdom of their wise men will perish' (Isa. 29:14). The biblical book of Proverbs explicitly states that natural revelation is not sufficient. Waltke says, 'Agur argues ... that Creation teaches the impossibility of attaining wisdom apart from special revelation (30:1–6).'[1] The book of Proverbs is also unique because it is divinely inspired and infallible (2 Tim. 3:16). Earthly wisdom is a fallible mix of truth and error, but God's wisdom can be fully relied upon because it is inerrant.

Most importantly, the book of Proverbs looks beyond Solomon to Christ, who is greater than Solomon (Matt. 12:41–42). While Solomon failed to live according to the wisdom God gave him, Jesus is Wisdom personified (8:22–31; 1 Cor. 1:24,30; Col. 2:3). It is in relation to Jesus Christ that we are able to live according to the wisdom about which Solomon writes. One of the objectives of this commentary is to take the reader beyond mere moralistic or pragmatic principles so that Christ can be seen on every page of the book of Proverbs.

Proverbs and the rest of the Old Testament

The book of Proverbs holds a special place in the Bible as the pinnacle of wisdom literature. Proverbs assumes and builds upon the precepts of the law and the admonitions of the prophets but goes beyond them in training the reader to live wisely in a very practical 'how to' way. Kidner writes, 'There are details of character small enough to escape the mesh of the law and the broadsides of the prophets, and yet decisive in personal dealings. Proverbs moves in this realm.'[2] One can read the historical narratives in the light of Proverbs to identify wise and foolish men and women and to learn from the outcomes of their lives.

Challenges in studying Proverbs

It is difficult to do a consecutive study or exposition of some sections of Proverbs

Chapters 1 through 9 and chapter 31 of Proverbs contain extended development of particular ideas and can be studied consecutively. The proverbs and sayings in chapters 10 through 30 are shorter and tend to jump from subject to subject. For this reason we will cover the content in those chapters topically, rather than going verse by verse.

The book of Proverbs does not explicitly proclaim the gospel

Proverbs is not evangelistic. Rather, it assumes its readers are already in covenant relationship with God. While the way of salvation in Christ is not explicitly spelled out, the appeals in the early chapters to turn away from folly to wisdom can be likened to calls to turn away from the world in repentance and turn to Christ in faith. Christ is the one 'in whom are hidden all the treasures of wisdom and knowledge' (Col. 2:3). Our understanding of Jesus is illuminated by the book of Proverbs, and our knowledge of Jesus illumines our understanding of Proverbs.

The book of Proverbs contains maxims, which are not the same as promises

Some have misread the book of Proverbs as a book of promises: if you raise your children correctly, they will be godly and never rebel (22:6); if you work hard, you will be rich (10:4); if you act wisely, you will live to a ripe old age

(3:2). The reality, however, is that some godly people have troubled kids, and some ungodly people have wonderful children (Ezek. 18:5–18); some hard-working Christians struggle to make ends meet; fools sometimes win the lottery; some godly folk die young of cancer or in a car accident; some who abuse substances defy the odds and live to a ripe old age.

The maxims of the book of Proverbs express general principles of how God runs the world. Those who live wisely are generally blessed with success in parenting and finances and with long life. The foolish, on the other hand, can generally expect trouble in this life because of their defiance of God's principles of wisdom. The exceptional cases do not nullify the wisdom of these sayings.

The book of Proverbs is primarily addressed to men

Some have been troubled because sons are repeatedly addressed in Proverbs with little reference to daughters. While men and women are spiritually equal (Gal. 3:28), God has assigned different roles to men and women. Men are to be the leaders in the home and in the church (Eph. 5:22–33; 1 Tim. 2:12–13; 3:1–7). The subordinate role of women is not demeaning, but rather women are like Christ, who willingly submitted to the headship of his Father (1 Cor. 11:3). Proverbs is written to young men as leaders in the covenant community and in their homes. The LORD addresses wives and daughters through their husbands, sons, and rulers under whose headship they fall. Therefore, the truths in Proverbs apply equally to women.

The book of Proverbs is for everyone!

1. Proverbs is written to prepare a young person who faces the challenges and opportunities of responsible adulthood.

2. Proverbs instructs parents in how to train their children (1:8).

3. Proverbs offers the basics of wisdom to those who are young and naive (1:4).

4. Proverbs deepens the understanding of those who are already wise (1:5).

5. Proverbs exposes the fool and the result of his or her arrogant rebellion (1:7*b*).

Background and summary

The title of the book (1:1) requires some explanation because the book of Proverbs contains more than just proverbs, and Solomon is not the only author.

The proverbs of Solomon (v. 1*a*)

What is a proverb? It almost seems easier to recognize one than to define one. The essential meaning of the Hebrew word translated 'proverbs' is 'similitude' or 'likeness'. Waltke defines a proverb as 'a short witty saying that gives you a standard by which you might judge your life'. He continues to describe a proverb as 'a comparison, an object lesson, a simple illustration, or a parable which exposes a fundamental reality about life'.[3] The objective of the book of Proverbs is to enable us to live successfully in relationship to God in the world he has created.

While this book is entitled 'Proverbs', the short pithy sayings do not begin until chapter 10. Chapters 1–9 are an extended appeal for the reader to seek wisdom.

Authorship (v. 1*b*)

This book is entitled 'The proverbs of Solomon the son of David, king of Israel.' It is appropriate that Solomon be named as the primary author of this book because he was the wisest man on earth (1 Kings 3:12; 4:29–34). Solomon spoke 3,000 proverbs (1 Kings 4:32), of which fewer than one-third are recorded. Solomon's proverbs make up the core of the book (10:1–22:16; 25:1–29:27). It is also likely that Solomon is the author of the introductory discourses (chs. 1–9). A careful examination of Proverbs reveals, however, that Solomon is not the only contributor (30:1; 31:1). Furthermore, we know that the final collection of wisdom in Proverbs was not completed until long after Solomon's death, because Proverbs 25:1 begins a collection of Solomon's sayings which were transcribed by the men of Hezekiah who lived around 700 BC (250 years after Solomon).

One great irony is that, in his later years, Solomon himself did not consistently pursue the wisdom taught in Proverbs, resulting in his life being ravaged by foolishness (1 Kings 11). Waltke remarks, 'Let it be noted that he constructed his own gibbet on which he impaled himself ([Prov.]19:27)—that is he ceased listening to his own instruction. Spiritual success today does not guarantee spiritual success tomorrow.'[4]

Setting

The book of Proverbs is set both in the home, where father and mother are instructing their beloved son (1:8), and in the palace, where a young man is being prepared for the responsibilities of leadership (31:1).

Divisions

The book of Proverbs is structured as follows:

1. Prologue (1:1–7)
2. A tenfold call to pursue wisdom (1:8–9:18)
3. The proverbs of Solomon (10:1–22:16)
4. Sayings of the wise (22:17–24:34)
5. More proverbs of Solomon (the Hezekian collection) (25:1–29:27)
6. The words of Agur (30:1–33)
7. The words of King Lemuel (or rather, of his mother) (31:1–9)
8. An acrostic of wifely excellence (31:10–31).

The approach of this commentary will be to examine sections 1, 2, and 8 in an expository fashion while dealing with the subjects raised in sections 3–7 topically.

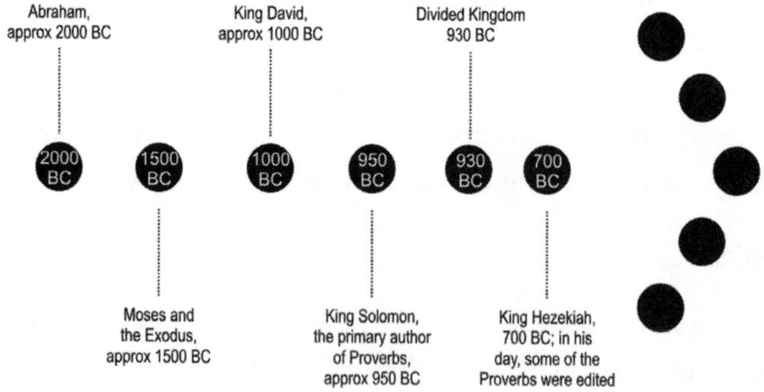

1 Wisdom and the fear of the LORD

(1:1–7)

The first seven verses serve as an introduction to the entire book of Proverbs. Verse 1 is the title; verses 2–6 express the twofold purpose of the book of Proverbs in one extended sentence; and verse 7 gives the motto of the book.

The purpose of the book of Proverbs (vv. 2–6)

Verse 2 summarizes the twofold purpose of Proverbs, which is further explained in verses 3–6: Proverbs equips the reader with moral skill for holy living, and Proverbs imparts mental discernment.

Proverbs will train God's people to live wisely (skilfully) (vv. 2*a*,3–5)

What is wisdom?

The essence of wisdom is skill, the ability to do a job. The same Hebrew word is used of the skilful workers who prepared Aaron's garments and of those who built the tabernacle and the temple (Exod. 28:3; 31:1–11; 1 Kings 7:14). Their exceptional ability to work with fabric and bronze was necessary and admirable (Prov. 22:29). Such skills were only obtained through hard work.

The goal of wisdom is that you might achieve a life of beauty and significance so that at the end of your days you will have accomplished something worthwhile and lasting.

The wisdom offered by the book of Proverbs is skill for living. Wisdom is not merely intellectual or academic; it is primarily moral. Solomon, as the wisest man on earth, demonstrated wisdom and skill as a naturalist, an administrator, and a judge (1 Kings 4:21–34; 3:6–28). The book of Proverbs teaches you how to live skilfully in every area of your life including family, finances, friendships, speech, and work. The goal of wisdom is that you might achieve a life of beauty and significance so that at the end of your days you will have accomplished something worthwhile and lasting. Jesus is the one who exemplifies wisdom, as he lived on earth with perfect skill. It is through Christ that we are made wise and gain the ability to live wisely.

Wisdom is gained through disciplined instruction

The word 'instruction' in verse 2*a* conveys the idea of learning through discipline. The same Hebrew word is used of the chastening imparted by a parent (13:24; 22:15) and of God training his covenant people through discipline (3:11; Deut. 11:2).

You were not born with wisdom. Nor do you automatically become wise as you grow older. The source of wisdom is God. Wisdom is gained through disciplined pursuit.

Because we are by nature foolish and lazy, we reject the hardship of learning by discipline (1:7*b*). We are wayward children who need to be brought under the rule of our heavenly Father (even if it is painful) for our own good. We need to learn to restrain our natural desires and to perform our duty. Those who are trained by discipline are successful.

Some time ago my family attended an organ concert at a local park. We were amazed at the virtuosity of the performer. What seemed effortless during the performance was the product of thousands of hours of hard work. The same can be said of others who have become skilful in sports, crafts, and trades.

Often we hear of people who had great talent, for example in sports or music, but fell far short of their potential because they did not have the discipline to fully develop their God-given abilities. Our author tells us from the beginning that if you want to be wise and successful in life you will have to work hard.

The nature of the training offered by God is not merely academic but is also highly practical. It is like the physician who perfects his craft, not merely through classroom learning, but also by practising medicine as a hospital intern. We apply the wisdom of Proverbs in the laboratory of life.

The student benefits from instruction (v. 3)

As you apply yourself to wisdom, you will 'receive instruction in wise behavior' (v. 3*a*). You will learn to act wisely in real-life situations instead of stumbling through life like a bull in a china shop, constantly saying and doing the wrong things. The Hebrew word translated 'wise behavior' is used of Abigail (1 Sam. 25:3), who dealt prudently with the threat posed to her household because of the folly of her husband Nabal (1 Sam. 25). Studying Proverbs will make you less like Nabal (Prov. 19:11) and more like Abigail. Such wisdom and prudence is also an attribute of our Lord Jesus that was expressed in his great work of saving his people ('Behold, my servant shall act wisely', Isa. 52:13, ESV).

The student will also learn 'righteousness, justice and equity' (v. 3*b*). 'Righteousness' is conformity to God's standard. The Hebrew word is used in Deuteronomy 25:13–15 in reference to the importance of not having two sets of weights in your bag that would enable you to cheat your neighbour by short-changing him or her when you sell and take too much when you buy. 'Justice and equity' are exercised by one who makes fair decisions. Such impartiality would have been essential for the future ruler to whom Proverbs was originally written.

Wisdom benefits the young and the simple (v. 4)

The teacher of wisdom gives 'prudence to the naive' (v. 4*a*). The Hebrew word translated 'naive' means open or gullible ('The naive believes everything', 14:15*a*). While our culture praises open-mindedness, it is not good to be open-minded when it comes to evil and error.

The first extended section of Proverbs (1:7–9:18) identifies two competing voices, Lady Wisdom and Madame Folly. The 'naive' person is vulnerable to the seductions of the world offered by Madame Folly and those connected with her. Wisdom will help the student to know the true facts of life so that he or she can recognize the dangers of the world and avoid falling into disastrous sin. Wisdom will enable you to discern between good and bad companions. You will be able to identify false values and beliefs.

The teacher also offers 'to the youth knowledge and discretion' (v. 4*b*). Young, inexperienced people are often aimless. They live only for the moment and do not plan for the future. It is sad to see people in their twenties and thirties who are drifting through life and achieving nothing. The wise young person will have 'discretion'—the ability to form plans so that important goals can be achieved.

Are you young? Do you realize you are naive? Do you sense you are drifting through life? There is hope for you. Pay heed to the wisdom God offers and you won't have to remain that way.

Those who are already wise will grow in wisdom (v. 5)

The book of Proverbs isn't merely for the young and immature. Those who are truly wise remain teachable and 'increase in learning' through continued disciplined study. God's wisdom is unfathomable. You can read through Proverbs hundreds of times with profit. As you go through the stages of life, you will gain new insights that go along with your experiences and help you live well.

You will also 'acquire wise counsel'. The Hebrew word translated 'wise counsel' was used of the ropes that would guide a ship. Most unbelievers are guided by worldly wisdom or personal feelings. Some seek mystical guidance through astrology and other forms of divination which are forbidden by Scripture (Deut. 18:9–14). No wonder their lives are in shambles! Proverbs warns against the counsel of fools and against following your own feelings ('There is a way which seems right to a man, but its end is the way of death', 14:12). The guidance offered by Proverbs is not mystical but rather moral, firmly grounded in truth and righteousness. One does not gain wisdom merely by being 'zapped' from above; rather, the godly person acquires wisdom for living through the disciplined study of God's Word, thereby establishing a pattern of wise choices in life.

Proverbs will impart mental discernment (vv. 2*b*,6)

You need insight into reality

Because of Adam's fall, our minds are corrupted by sin. Our confusion is compounded because we live in a postmodern world that denies the existence of absolute truth and encourages each person to construct his or her own reality.

The essential meaning of the word translated 'discern' in verse 2*b* (translated 'understand' in verse 6*a*) is to 'distinguish between two things'. A person who likes chocolates with nuts will examine a box of chocolates and seek those that fit his or her taste, rejecting those with soft centres. Solomon prayed, 'So give Your servant an understanding heart to judge Your people to discern between good and evil' (1 Kings 3:9*a*). Hebrews 5:14 speaks of the mature 'who because of practice have their senses trained to discern good and evil'. Discernment will help you decide which teachers to embrace and which ones you should steer clear of because of their unbiblical doctrine. Discernment will help you to distinguish between what is true and false, what is right and wrong in culture (e.g. movies, television, education, etc.). You won't have to live with the perpetual uncertainty of postmodern worldly philosophy but instead will have confidence that you know the truth.

For example, a Christian family that had been studying Proverbs together in their evening devotions once found themselves driving through an impoverished area of their city where they saw many street people. One of the children commented with discernment, 'Poor is he who works with a negligent hand, but the hand of the diligent makes rich' (10:4).

You need insight into God's Word

You could hand me a Korean Bible and I could pass my eyes over its characters, but it would do me no good. You might offer a nine-year-old an advanced physics textbook, but he or she is not likely to grasp its content. For the natural man, the Bible itself is foolishness (1 Cor. 2:14). With the help of the Holy Spirit, your disciplined study of Proverbs will help you develop important skill in understanding the wisdom contained in God's Word.

You need to understand the figures of speech in Proverbs

The book of Proverbs contains a variety of literary devices ('a proverb and a figure, the words of the wise and their riddles', v. 6). There are parables, aphorisms, and sayings. Some of the proverbs use humour: 'The sluggard buries his hand in the dish, but will not even bring it back to his mouth' (19:25). Many of the Proverbs employ parallelism, sometimes synonymous (restating the same point) and at other times antithetical (making a contrast). You must read carefully or you will make errors in interpretation.

Studying the book of Proverbs will sharpen your mind

You may have already read Proverbs and appreciated the practical wisdom offered. I want to challenge you to go deeper so you will better understand the value of wisdom and how it is attained. The book of Proverbs offers you an education unsurpassed by any institution of higher learning. Through disciplined study you will learn both how to think and how to live well.

The credo for the book of Proverbs (v. 7)

Proverbs is not merely a 'how to' book. Your quest for wisdom begins with the 'fear of the LORD' who is in covenant relationship with his redeemed people (v. 7*a*). The use of the covenant name of God, LORD (*YHWH* in the Hebrew), ties Proverbs to the rest of the Bible. Because we are spiritual children of Abraham by faith (Gal. 3:29), we are in covenant relationship with the LORD, which means that Proverbs, along with the rest of the Old Testament, is written for us.

The LORD is the source of all true knowledge and wisdom. Wisdom is an attribute of God: 'With Him are wisdom and might; to Him belong counsel and understanding' (Job 12:13). His wisdom is displayed in his works: 'It is He who made the earth by His power, who established the world by His wisdom; and by His understanding He has stretched out the heavens' (Jer. 10:12; see also Prov. 8:22–31). Wisdom is imparted to men through God's Word: 'The law of the LORD is perfect, restoring the soul; the testimony of the LORD is sure, making wise the simple' (Ps. 19:7).

You cannot discern the true nature of life and the world apart from the Lord who is the root of all knowledge.

God imparts wisdom to those who seek him: 'If any of you lacks wisdom, let him ask of God, who gives to all generously and without reproach, and it will be given to him' (James 1:5). The early chapters of Proverbs plead with the naive reader to earnestly pursue wisdom. The New Testament reveals that the ultimate expression of wisdom is found in Jesus Christ (1 Cor. 1:30–31).

You cannot discern the true nature of life and the world apart from the LORD who is the root of all knowledge. The one who tries to be wise apart from God is a branch cut off from the root. For this reason, only the godly are truly wise. The humble workman or the faithful homemaker may be wiser than the Professor of Philosophy at Oxford or Harvard.

What does it mean to fear the LORD?

To fear God is to regard God with reverent awe. He alone is holy, awesome, and glorious (Isa. 6:3). He is worthy of our respect. Because God is righteous, we should be concerned about the consequences of displeasing him. Our fear is not one which leaves us cowering and terrified but rather is like the respect a son should have towards his father. The fear of God leads to wise and pure living: 'By the fear of the LORD one keeps away from evil' (Prov. 16:6*b*).

To fear God is to submit to him, turning from self-assertion and evil: 'Do not be wise in your own eyes; fear the LORD and turn away from evil' (3:7). We are not autonomous beings, free to assert our own will and decide what is right for us. We must acknowledge the LORD's sovereign moral governance of the universe. We should be open to his training and correction and trust that his way is always best. To fear God is to know God. To know God is to have life (19:23*a*). When you fear God, you no longer fear men (29:25).

The fear of the LORD is not a beginning like the first stage of a rocket which is cast aside after it has served its purpose. Rather, the fear of the LORD is the beginning of wisdom in the same way in which a foundation is the beginning of a house: everything that comes after the foundation is built upon it.

Don't be a fool! Fools despise wisdom and instruction (v. 7*b*)

Proverbs contrasts two types of individuals—the wise and the foolish. Foolishness is not merely a mental defect. Rather, folly is a moral deficiency which leads to all kinds of disasters and sins in life. Fools lack sense, and they lack the sense to know that they lack sense. Fools are unteachable because they are proud. 'Do not be wise in your own eyes; fear the LORD and turn away from evil' (3:7). They reject God's wisdom and they hate discipline. A fool ends up wasting his or her life, ultimately coming to ruin (1:30–32).

Conclusion

What do you seek? We live in a world full of fools playing games. They imagine that their accumulation of fame, fortune, and pleasure will make them winners. In spite of our investment of billions in educating our young people, test scores are down and juvenile crime is rising. Some students are learning facts but remain foolish. Spurgeon writes, 'To know is not to be wise. Many men know a great deal and are the greater fools for it. There is no fool as great as a knowing fool.'[5] Our young people are being taught materialism and hedonism instead of the fear of the LORD. Ultimate moral and spiritual values are excluded from the classroom. Parents need to heed the message of Proverbs by taking responsibility for the training of their children in wisdom.

Sadly, many churches are failing to impact on our culture because they are pandering to these misplaced man-centred values of the world rather than proclaiming the fear of the LORD. Sometimes Proverbs is taught merely as a book of practical tips for earthly success so that people can win at the game of life. But wisdom begins with the fear of the LORD, and it grows in personal relationship with him. We need churches that unashamedly declare the truth of God to believers who treasure wisdom.

God's offer of wisdom to all who seek it from him is not merely a maxim; it is a promise. Skill for living does not come upon you suddenly but grows as you apply yourself to understanding and applying the wisdom of God contained in his Word. Ultimately, you can only become wise through Christ, who both embodies wisdom and makes his people wise. Pursue wisdom!

FOR FURTHER STUDY

1. Other than Solomon, what biblical examples of wise men and women can you think of? (See, for example, Gen. 41:39.)
2. Name some biblical examples of fools. (See 1 Sam. 25.)
3. Can you think of people who have been characterized by wisdom and foolishness at different times? (See 1 Kings 11.)

TO THINK ABOUT AND DISCUSS

1. What is a proverb?
2. What is the twofold goal of Proverbs (see 1:2)?
3. What is wisdom? How can we impart wisdom to others?
4. What is the relationship between wisdom and discipline (see 1:3)? What kind of hard work is required to gain wisdom?
5. What does it mean to fear God (see 1:7)? How can we demonstrate the fear of God at work and in our homes? How is it evident that our culture has lost the fear of God? How can we teach our children to fear God?
7. Why would the attaining of worldly wisdom, apart from the fear of the LORD, leave you a fool?

2 Two invitations with one moral

(1:8–33)

The early chapters of Proverbs call upon the reader to make a choice between the voice of folly and the voice of wisdom. Folly invites you to join a murderous gang; Wisdom cries out in the streets, pleading with men to turn away from foolishness and enjoy true life.

Wisdom begins at home (vv. 8–9)

If the fear of the LORD is at the root of our quest for wisdom, family instruction is the trunk from which wisdom grows. The introductory formula 'my son' is used ten times in the first nine chapters (1:8; 2:1; 3:1; 4:1,10,20; 5:1; 6:1,20; 7:1) and marks out major sections of Wisdom's appeal.

In Western culture, the primary influences in the lives of young people include their teachers, their schoolmates, and the entertainment industry. But God's plan is that parents are to be the primary teachers of wisdom. In Proverbs we have a beautiful picture of a godly family at work. It is assumed that the parents willingly take on their duty to instruct their children and that they carry it out well. A major purpose of the book of Proverbs is to prepare a young man to wisely and effectively assume the responsibilities of adult life.

While the best-known proverbs may speak about the rod of discipline, loving parental instruction is even more important (v. 8; 4:1–9). Such was the expectation of families under the Old Covenant: 'These words, which I am commanding you today, shall be on your heart. You shall teach them diligently to your sons and shall talk of them when you sit in your house and when you walk by the way and when you lie down and when you rise up' (Deut. 6:6–7). The duty of parents to teach their children God's Word is reaffirmed under the New Covenant (Eph. 6:4). Both father and mother have a vital role in training their children (Prov. 1:8; 4:3–4; 31:1,26; see also 2 Tim. 1:5; 3:14–15).

Children are exhorted to listen respectfully to both of their parents. Wise sons and daughters are excellent listeners. They want their parents to be the primary influence in their lives. They listen both to their mothers and to their fathers, not playing them off against each other. 'A fool rejects his father's discipline, but he who regards reproof is sensible' (15:5). Children whose parents are striving to train them in wisdom should thank God!

Often people will judge a child by his or her outward appearance. But according to Proverbs, it is the adornment of parental wisdom that makes a child attractive (1:9). Both the Old and New Testaments affirm God's blessing upon those who honour their parents (Exod. 20:12; Eph. 6:3). Jesus honoured and obeyed his earthly parents when he was a child (Luke 2:51).

> ... parents are fully responsible for training their children and for the influences under which they allow their children to come.

Proverbs warns us that the world is full of foolish and destructive influences, including substitute 'families' that attempt to usurp the role God has given to parents. Christian parents who would never think of sending their children to Islamic schools send them to secular schools that are steeped in secular humanism and postmodernism. Then, when they return home, the kids come under other foolish influences from television, music, and the Internet. This is not to say that every parent must shelter and isolate his or her child from every influence outside the home. The point is that parents are fully responsible for training their children and for the influences under which they allow their children to come. Many parents are so busy trying to provide the best material things for their children that they abdicate their responsibility to properly train them.

Refuse the appeal of ungodly companions (vv. 10–19)

The wise father of Proverbs portrays the world according to its true (and dangerous) nature. He also warns us of how the wicked can make sin appear attractive. The Bible never denies that sometimes sin is, in the short run, pleasurable. As with a scorpion, the sting is in the tail. Some parents shelter their children from the world so much that their young ones are naive and vulnerable. Proverbs helps parents prepare their children for the allurements of the world and train them in how to resist evil.

The enticement of moral misfits (vv. 10–14)

Our instruction in wisdom begins with a dramatic description of a young man being invited to join a violent gang. It reads as if it could have been written today about temptations facing our young people. Those who are of the world are trying to seduce our children into substance abuse, crime, and immorality. Many worldly people take particular pleasure in luring and ruining the righteous and their offspring.

The gang promises excitement, financial gain ('We will find all kinds of precious wealth, we will fill our houses with spoil', v. 13) and community ('Throw in your lot with us, we shall all have one purse', 1:14). The wise person is able to resist because he or she sees beyond the allurements of sin to recognize the true nature of the wicked and the end result of their folly.

These criminals promote senseless violence and have no regard for human life (vv. 11–12). They crave the feeling of power they enjoy with a weapon in their hand before a cowering victim. 'We are a force to be reckoned with. We aren't afraid of anyone.' They have a sense of invincibility. They spur one another on to further exploits of evil. They are hard and detached from the reality of what they are doing and the suffering and harm they bring upon others.

They want easy money (v. 13). Proverbs has much to say about God's way of earning money through hard work (10:4). These people think they can circumvent the system and, through theft, enjoy the fruit of other men's labours.

They offer a substitute family (v. 14). There is a perverse brotherhood among criminals. They are loyal to the gang. Young people who do not have a sense of belonging at home are vulnerable to gangs who welcome them. Gang members are willing to smoke, drink, abuse drugs, steal, or even kill so they can belong. The increase in gang membership and the resultant rise in violence can be directly attributed to the breakdown of the family.

> Young people need to beware of friends who offer identity or demand loyalty that competes with that of their families.

Young people need to beware of friends who offer identity or demand loyalty that competes with that of their families. Many parents are contributing to the delinquency of their children by failing to be engaged in their lives and by tolerating or even financially enabling sinful behaviour. Children of immigrants can be especially vulnerable to gangs because their families have lost much of the identity they had in the old country. The parents are struggling to survive in the new culture and may not have much time for their children. Plus, Mom and Dad don't fit in. Sinful peers offer identity and community that such kids crave.

All parents need to devote time and effort to building

family relationships, doing whatever it takes to make the family the primary place of training and socialization for their children. They must be willing to make sacrifices of time, money, and careers to fulfil the responsibilities God has given them. What does it profit their children if they gain all the material blessings they crave but grow up to be fools?

If you follow evil companions, you will reap destruction (vv. 15–19)

Fools consider the short-term benefits of sin but fail to consider the long-term consequences. Their outrageously evil acts cry out for judgement (v. 16). They may not care about the harm they cause to others, but there is a just God who will ensure that they receive what they deserve.

Our author illustrates their stupidity in verses 17–18. Even a bird knows better than to step into an obvious trap. Violent gang members have less foresight and are more foolish than dumb birds. While they plot the destruction of others, they actually are devising their own doom. In a sense, they are caught in their own trap, like Haman who was executed on the gallows he had prepared for Mordecai (Esth. 7). Those who choose a life of crime ruin their own lives. Sooner or later they will be caught and punished. Substance abusers often wind up addicted, addled, and homeless. The life expectancy of gang members on the street is short (v. 19). They see their friends die young, yet they do not learn.

Choose your companions wisely

An implicit message in this early section of Proverbs is a reminder of the influence your friends will have upon your character and your reputation. 'Do not be deceived: "Bad company corrupts good morals"' (1 Cor. 15:33). It is also important that you choose your heroes carefully. The media makes much of the scandalous personal lives of celebrities. It is troubling to see young people imitating them in the way they dress and act.

A young person's primary social group and influence should be the family, not peers. He or she should gain a sense of belonging and community at home. Anyone who tries to pull anyone away from his or her family is an enemy. Wisdom begins at home.

Heed the appeal of Wisdom before it is too late (vv. 20–33)

A second voice invites the young person to an entirely different pursuit.

Wisdom calls out to you (vv. 20–23)

Wisdom is personified in the early chapters of Proverbs as a woman who is placed in stark contrast to Madame Folly, who would seduce and destroy you. She is the soul's true lover and bride who should be prized and embraced (4:6–8). She is a tree of life (3:18). Here she sounds like one of the prophets appealing to God's people to turn before it is too late. She offers great blessing to those who listen but warns of terrifying judgement upon those who reject her. She does not keep her message secret but goes into every public place (vv. 20–21) in order to get the widest possible hearing. Her voice is loud, even shrill and piercing, because of the urgency of her appeal.

Wisdom appeals to four different categories of fools (v. 22)

These four types of men are important throughout Proverbs. Each type of person requires different treatment according to his character. The New Testament also reminds us that we need to be sensitive to the different kinds of people to whom we seek to minister (1 Thes. 5:14).

The naive is committed neither to good nor evil (vv. 4,10, 22; 8:5; 27:12). Because he has not devoted himself to wisdom, he is vulnerable to seduction by Madame Folly (7:7; 9:4). Because he has not yet given himself over to folly, there is hope that he will turn to wisdom before it is too late (9:4–6).

The fool (Hebrew *keciyl*) has rejected wisdom and has become morally insensitive. He is so occupied with the things of the world that the things of God are of no concern to him. His bad character and behaviour bring overwhelming grief to his parents (15:20). To try to reason with a fool is a waste of time (26:3–5).

A stronger word for *fool* (Hebrew *eviyl)* is used in Proverbs 1:7. This man is not merely dull like the *keciyl*; he loves folly and 'despises wisdom and instruction'. Such fools must be allowed to face the consequences of their folly (10:21).

The scoffer is on the faculty of the graduate School of Folly. He is the 'free-thinking' cynic who mocks at God, sin, and judgement. He is hardened against any reproof (9:7–8). He is not content with his own folly but recruits followers as he strives to undermine wisdom by drawing the naive away from God. Many of the elite in media, entertainment, and academia fall into the category of scoffer. Scoffers are to be avoided (22:10) and we should be wary of allowing such people to influence us (Ps. 1:1).

Wisdom promises blessing to those who repent (v. 23)

There is hope, however, that fools can change if they will only heed the voice of Wisdom, who offers to pour out her spirit upon the listener. Who would refuse such a wonderful and gracious invitation? Do you realize that you have been a fool? If so, you are well on your way to wisdom. Seek wisdom from God who will not refuse you (James 1:5).

If you reject Wisdom's appeal, you will reap calamity (vv. 24–32)

God's patience with fools who refuse to listen to Wisdom's voice will finally run out (vv. 24–25). Judgement will come suddenly and unexpectedly like a storm. Wisdom will have the last laugh, as those who mocked wisdom will themselves become the object of mocking (vv. 26–27; see also 3:34; Ps. 2:4; Deut. 28:63).

On the Day of Judgement, the wicked will have passed the point of no return (vv. 28–30). Those under God's judgement in hell will not be able to seek wisdom or call out to God in repentance but rather will merely cry out for deliverance from the terrible consequences of their folly (Luke 16:24). The knowledge of their refusal to listen when they had the opportunity will compound their misery (Isa. 66:4). They will reap what they have sown (Prov. 1:31–32; Gal. 6:7–8).

Those who seek wisdom are secure (v. 33)

Some people wear a Saint Christopher medal, thinking it will protect them from danger. Our text teaches that it is the one who is adorned by wisdom who is safe even on the Day of Judgement.

Conclusion: The voice of Wisdom is the voice of God

The cry of Wisdom in Proverbs recalls how, under the Old Covenant, God cried out to Israel through the law and the prophets, promising blessing for obedience and judgement to those who refuse, to pay heed to his voice (Deut. 28:63–68).

Jesus is wisdom incarnate

Under the New Covenant, God speaks to his people through our Lord Jesus, in whom is the fullness of wisdom (1 Cor. 1:30). The urgent pleas of Wisdom remind us of Jesus, who is full of love and compassion for sinners. He pleaded with the lost (Matt. 23:37; 11:28–30; compare Prov. 1:20–21). Jesus pours out his Spirit upon those who seek him (John 7:37–39; compare Prov. 1:23). He gives life to all who come to him (John 1:4; 3:15–16; compare Prov. 3:18). Jesus also warned that the season of mercy will pass when he comes to judge those who reject him (Matt. 23:37–39; 21:33–44; compare Prov. 1:24–27). Those who trust him will be safe on the Day of Judgement (Heb. 2:15; John 10:28; compare Prov. 1:33).

You are the voice of wisdom to a foolish world

In this age in which we await Jesus' return, we Christians are the voice of Christ (Wisdom) to our foolish age (Rom. 10:18). We are not to keep our lamp under a bushel but have been sent by him to go to the public square and plead with the naive and the foolish to turn to Christ (Matt. 28:18–20). We, like Lady Wisdom and Jesus, may be rejected by many, but some will turn and gain life (Isa. 55:11; Acts 13:48).

Are you wise?

It may be that you are reading this while yet unconverted. God appeals to you today (Isa. 1:18–20). He calls out to you through the Bible, through the preaching of his Word, through Christian friends and family members and through your conscience. God graciously offers full forgiveness of your sins, transformation of your life, and everlasting fellowship with him, all through Christ's work on the cross. Turn to him today while his gracious hand is extended to you. When the Day of Judgement comes, it will be too late, but he is ready now to hear and answer your prayers for grace and wisdom. Today is the day of salvation (2 Cor. 6:2).

FOR FURTHER STUDY

1. How did unwise companions influence Amnon and Rehoboam (see 2 Sam. 13; 1 Kings 12)?
2. Describe the four categories of people to whom Wisdom appeals (see 1:22 and 1:7*b*). Do you know people who fall into each of these categories?

TO THINK ABOUT AND DISCUSS

1. Why do kids join gangs? What can be done to strengthen the identity a child feels with his or her family?
2. Why are we tempted at times to listen to Folly? How can we cultivate a mindset of rejecting Folly's invitations?
3. How does Wisdom relate to the law and the prophets?
4. In what sense is the voice of Wisdom the voice of Jesus?
5. Have you seen situations in which both Wisdom and Folly were crying out to someone? How did he or she respond?

3 The blessings of wisdom

(2:1–22)

In ancient times, people often sought their fortunes by seeking buried treasure. In our day, people might seek earthly treasure by playing the stock market. The book of Proverbs calls upon us to search for wisdom as a hidden treasure.

The benefits of wisdom far outweigh what one can receive from earthly riches. True wisdom is not merely intellectual knowledge but a transformation of character. Proverbs 1 has entreated us to pursue wisdom; Proverbs 2 tells us how to pursue wisdom (vv. 1–4) and then sets forth the great benefits of wisdom (vv. 5–22).

Earnestly seek wisdom (vv. 1–4)

Some people read verses like James 1:5 ('But if any of you lacks wisdom, let him ask of God, who gives to all generously and without reproach, and it will be given to him') and imagine that God simply zaps us with the quality of wisdom when we ask him. Proverbs explains that God grants wisdom by means of a process. In order to gain this treasure, you must exert effort in digging deep for it. The word 'if' occurs three times in verses 1–4, indicating specific conditions for the blessings that are promised in verses 5 and following.

Be receptive to wisdom (vv. 1–2)

Does your soul thirst after knowledge? Some people are hard, like the path in Jesus' parable of the soils. God's Word just bounces off them. Others are like the good soil that held the seed fast and bore much fruit (Luke 8:15). In the previous chapter, Wisdom pleaded with you to pay attention to her. Have you heeded her cry? The fact that you are taking time to read this book indicates you have a desire to gain more wisdom from God's Word.

Merely going through the motions of religion will not make you wise.

Do you treasure God's Word in your soul? In 1849 thousands of men were willing to leave their comfortable homes to travel to far-away California, where they lived in tents and spent day after day in back-breaking labour, all because they hoped to find a few nuggets of gold. Would that we approached our personal Bible reading, the sermons we hear at church, and Bible classes with the same fervour. Merely going through the motions of religion will not make you wise. You must fully exert yourself and dig deeply.

Do you actively memorize Scripture? In so doing, you fill your mind, like a vault, with wisdom. Some of the chapters of Proverbs seem to have been arranged to make memorization easier. For example, chapter 2 has twenty-two verses, corresponding to the twenty-two letters of the Hebrew alphabet. We learn from Jesus' encounter with Satan in the wilderness that the ability to recall Scripture from memory can be very useful in times of trial. We can be like him as we not only memorize the Word but also internalize its teachings.

Are you a good listener? To show up in church sleepy or distracted shows a disrespectful attitude towards God and his Word. The fool sleeps and daydreams in church. His lackadaisical attitude towards the Word of God contributes to the hardening of his heart (Heb. 2:1; 3:15). Would you like to be more attentive? Prepare to hear God's Word by reviewing the text to be covered and then getting a good rest the night before. Take notes during the sermon so you will retain what you heard. Humbly receive God's Word (James 1:21). This also applies in the context of family instruction as children should listen attentively to their parents, whom God has appointed to make them wise.

Earnestly pursue wisdom (vv. 3–4)

While verses 1–2 speak of our receptivity to wisdom, verses 3–4 declare how we ought to proactively pursue wisdom. As I write this, tens of thousands of people are gathering at a nearby stadium in the first phase of the *American Idol* auditions. Many will do virtually anything to attain their goal of being a famous pop star. We see many others pursuing financial fortunes with the same zeal. We should pursue wisdom with even greater fervour.

Cry out, in prayer, to God for understanding (v. 3)

Because of sin, we are mentally and morally blind. We need the Holy Spirit to give us the light and sight of understanding. Without the Spirit's help, you can't correctly apprehend God's truth (1 Cor. 2:14). Do you prayerfully seek God's help as you study the Bible and attend the preaching of the Word? Plead with God to open your eyes that you might see wonderful things in his Word (Ps. 119:18). Just as a hungry baby insistently cries with a need that only the mother can satisfy, so we should 'like newborn babies long for the pure milk of the word, that by it [we] may grow in respect to salvation' (1 Peter 2:2). Have you said in your heart, 'I really want to know God'? The fact that you desire wisdom is evidence of his working in your life to help you gain wisdom.

The fact that you desire wisdom is evidence of his working in your life to help you gain wisdom.

Search, through diligent study, for wisdom as treasure (v. 4)

When I was in college, I had the privilege of meeting Ronald Reagan and getting his autograph. After having moved several times over many years, I realized that my prized autograph had become lost. I searched my home and my parents' home. I tore through old drawers and boxes, investing dozens of hours on my quest. Finally, after my not having seen the autograph for over fifteen years, my father discovered it buried among some papers in his safe. I rejoiced like the woman who found her lost coin (Luke 15:9).

Our author says that we should search for wisdom in the way in which I searched for my souvenir. In verse 3 he tells us to pray, but prayer alone is not enough! Just as we pray for our daily bread but then expect God to provide through the means of our hard work, so we should pray for wisdom and then trust God to provide by means of our diligently pursuing the wisdom for which we pray. Just as the gold miner had to use a pick to dig deep for the gold found in California, so you must be prepared to dig deeply into God's Word. Slow down and meditate upon what you read. Use the tools God has given you (i.e. a concordance and Bible commentaries like this one) to dig deeper into the Scriptures.

This single-minded pursuit of wisdom is what James refers to in 1:6–8 of his epistle. The double-minded man who says he wants wisdom but doesn't earnestly pursue it will not receive anything from the LORD. The person who pursues wisdom wholeheartedly will be abundantly blessed.

Keep seeking wisdom

You never 'arrive' when it comes to the practical knowledge of God's Word. Keep listening, praying, and pursuing. If you aren't growing in wisdom, it is probably because you have not been seeking and treasuring wisdom as you should. Perhaps you have valued earthly things, which are like fool's gold, above the lasting treasures of God, which will bring you joy and success forever.

Seek wisdom in Christ

Solomon was the wisest man on earth, and people came from great distances to hear his wisdom. How much more should we seek wisdom from him who is far greater than Solomon (Luke 11:31)! Be receptive to his Word (John 8:31–32). Pray that God will give you of his fullness. Actively seek him (Col. 3:1).

Wisdom will bless you in many ways (vv. 5–22)

If you fulfil the conditions listed in verses 1–4, you will enjoy the rich blessings from wisdom that are enumerated in verses 5–22.

You will know God personally (vv. 5–8)

Through wisdom comes a proper relationship with God. You will fear the LORD, experiencing his awesome transcendence. You also will enjoy a personal, intimate knowledge of and fellowship with him (v. 5). The wise man realizes that wisdom is not to be found within himself, as some psychologists and philosophers would teach, for 'he who trusts in his own heart is a fool' (28:26). Nor can we trust in the wisdom of mere men (Col. 2:8,3; Eccles. 1:18). God is the source of all wisdom and gives generously to those who seek him (v. 6). This wisdom of God is not subjective but is objectively revealed in the Scriptures. Nor is wisdom merely information or direction. Wisdom from God produces quality of life and security (v. 8; see also 3:17).

Wisdom will transform you as a person (vv. 9–11)

When wisdom enters your heart (v. 10*a*), you will become a changed person. You will be able to discern right from wrong (v. 9*a*). You will make decisions that are wise and just (v. 9*b*). You will enjoy success in the important relationships in your life. You will have confidence that your choices are sound.

You will have a taste for what is best ('knowledge will be pleasant to your soul', 2:10*b*). All my life I have been told that green vegetables, such as Brussels sprouts, are good for me. I confess, however, that I have no desire to eat them. Imagine if I were to wake up tomorrow and my desire for a chicken dish had disappeared and been replaced with a longing for mounds of Brussels sprouts. Most would say that I had experienced a miraculous transformation of taste. In the same way, wisdom gives us a new and growing desire to share God's good taste for truth which has become pleasant to our souls. The prospect of Bible study becomes attractive to us, like the smell of freshly baked bread. Would that each of us would be as repulsed by folly and attracted to wisdom as we ought to be!

Wisdom also gives us discernment. Just as a mother has a trained nose to sniff the milk in the refrigerator to know if it is spoiled, wisdom will enable us to distinguish between good and evil. We won't need hundreds of legalistic rules for every situation; we will have an inner sense to discern what is best.

This is the training our children need. It is not enough for them to hear Bible stories and memorize verses. Why do many children from Christian families turn from the faith when they leave the home? Because, while they received the Word of God on an external level, they never internalized what they were taught. Education is about training your children's tastes to discern between good and evil and love wisdom.

Wisdom will deliver you from dangerous people (vv. 12–22)

Proverbs seeks to prepare us to live in the real world, where there are many threats to our virtue. The latter half of Proverbs 2 tells how wisdom protects the young man from dangerous men and women.

Wisdom will protect you from evil men (vv. 12–15)

When teens get into trouble with the law, you will often hear their parents say, 'My kid is a good kid. He just got in with a bad crowd.' We have already seen in 1:8–19 the warning about the harm that peer pressure can do to a young person. Those who are wise learn to recognize and stay away from evil characters and their wayward paths. John Bunyan's classic, *Pilgrim's Progress*, describes dangerous characters such as Talkative, Mr Worldly Wiseman, Mr Money-love, and Mr Hold-the-world. It is hard to spend much time with such men and yet emerge unscathed.

You can recognize these men by their speech ('perverse things', v. 12*b*), their behaviour ('who leave the paths of uprightness to walk in the ways of darkness … whose paths are crooked', vv. 13,15*a*), and their desires/tastes ('who delight in doing evil and rejoice in the perversity of evil', v. 14). They are deceitful and can appear very smooth (v. 15*b*).

They are completely without moral illumination (John 3:19–20), and their path leads to the City of Destruction.

The wise person will be repulsed by their values, their characters, and their lifestyles and will stay far away from them (1 Cor. 15:33).

Wisdom will deliver you from loose women (vv. 16–19)

Here our author raises the subject of sexual temptation, which is a major concern in the book of Proverbs and one to which we will devote an entire chapter. Sexual sin is a rampant problem, not only in the world, but even among professing Christians who fall into lust, fornication, and adultery. The man caught in the grip of sexual sin asks, 'Why can't I gain victory over lust?' Our author summarizes in a few short verses how wisdom can set you free from lust. The key is that you must see the immoral woman (or man) as God sees her (or him). Such truth is life-transforming.

1. *You need to be aware of her methods (v. 16*b*).* Proverbs never hides the fact that sin can be appealing. The Strange Woman is seductive, offering charm, outward beauty, and sensual pleasures. She knows every trick in the book. She is a flatterer. She is confident she can wrap the naive young man around her little finger. He doesn't realize she is spreading a net for his feet (29:5).

2. *You need to recognize her true character (vv. 16*a*,17).* Wouldn't it be nice if a man could put on a pair of glasses that would make immoral and immodest women look hideously ugly? Proverbs offers you such spiritual spectacles. Wisdom enables you to look beyond the Strange Woman's outward beauty and seductiveness to see the ugliness of her character.

By wisdom you will be repulsed by her. She is called the 'strange woman' (v. 16*a*) because she is a stranger who doesn't belong. She is not the wife with whom you have a covenant relationship but rather an outsider who threatens your family and your life. She is also a quitter, one who 'leaves the companion of her youth' (v. 17*a*). She wasn't faithful to her first husband, and she won't be true to you. She doesn't form lasting allegiances to anyone. The same is true for the adulterous man. When a man leaves his wife for his secretary, why is the secretary shocked when, five years later, he leaves her for someone else? Ultimately, the Strange Woman's disloyalty is towards God (v. 17*b*), whose covenant she 'forgets' (deliberately ignores). Every marriage is a covenant made before God, who hates divorce (Mal. 2:14; Matt. 19:6*b*). A covenant commitment made before God means nothing to the adulteress because she does not fear God. Sadly, this link between spiritual fidelity and the fear of God reminds us of Solomon, whose attraction to 'strange' (foreign and idolatrous) women led to his spiritual unfaithfulness to God (1 Kings 11:1–8).

A covenant commitment made before God means nothing to the adulteress because she does not fear God.

Young people should realize that a person who would be disloyal to God by engaging in sexual immorality before marriage cannot be trusted to be faithful after marriage. Men should recognize that a woman who displays her body for all to see is being unfaithful to God by offering what should belong to a husband to anyone who is willing to look (or pay). This is not a woman who will be an asset, one whom you can trust with your name and reputation in the community. You can't bring a woman like this home to your mother. Nor do you want her raising your children. Those who are wise have their 'glasses' on and are repulsed by 'strange women' who mock God's design for sexuality.

3. *You need to realize where she will lead you (vv. 18–19,22).* My dear wife is in a never-ending battle with gophers that dig up our back garden. She puts out gopher bait, which consists of grain containing tasteless poison. Her expectation is that the gophers will see the tasty corn, consume it, and die. In the same way, the loose woman appears attractive. In reality, she is a *femme fatale* (deadly woman). If you take the bait, you will die. Our author paints a vivid picture similar to a scene from a horror movie: 'Her house sinks down to death' (v. 18*a*).

You will never gain when you defy the LORD.

The Sirens of Greek mythology appeared as beautiful women who used irresistible music to seduce unwitting sailors to turn towards their island. Then their ships would crash on hidden reefs, and the Sirens would eat them. I have counselled many men who have destroyed their families and ruined their personal lives through immorality. Most deceived themselves, thinking, 'I can have a little fun and my wife will never have to know.' They thought they could deviate from God's path and quickly return. Proverbs warns,

'None who go to her return again, nor do they reach the paths of life' (v. 19). God judges sexual sin (v. 22; Heb. 13:4). You will never gain when you defy the LORD. Sexual sin is especially heinous because marital faithfulness is a picture of our covenant faithfulness to God (Ezek. 23:35; James 4:4).

4. *When you see the adulteress as she really is, she is no longer a threat to you.* The man who struggles with lust shouldn't merely pray for deliverance, hoping that God will zap away all his sinful desires: the key to sexual purity is having the wisdom to see the immoral woman as God sees her. Putting on the glasses of wisdom will help you to recognize the Sirens before it is too late, whether you see them at the beach, on the Internet, on television, or in the marketplace. You will be repulsed as you realize their true character and the consequences of being seduced by them.

Wisdom will keep you safe (vv. 20–21)

By wisdom you will have good companions, as opposed to evil men and strange women (v. 20*a*). By wisdom you will walk in righteousness (v. 20*b*). The result will be security in God's kingdom (v. 21; see also Ps. 37:29; Matt. 5:5).

Christ offers true joy and happiness

Greek mythology describes how Odysseus and his men were able to get past the island of the Sirens. The men put beeswax in their ears so they wouldn't hear the Sirens' song, and Odysseus had himself bound to the mast so that he couldn't jump overboard to join the Sirens. Some people try to resist temptation in the same way. There was one other adventurer who escaped the Sirens. Orpheus played more beautiful music that drowned out the Siren song, enabling Jason's ship to slip by their island. Proverbs reveals the true nature of the immoral woman and the consequences of being seduced by her. Proverbs also takes a positive approach to purity. Lady Wisdom, who is a personification of Christ, is more beautiful and sings a sweeter song than Madame Folly. With her a man can find true joy and fulfilment. Seek Christ, in whom are the treasures of wisdom (Col. 2:3; Prov. 2:4). He is the path to life (John 14:6; Prov. 2:20). In him you will find safety and security.

FOR FURTHER STUDY

1. How does Proverbs 2 point to Christ? (See Col. 2:3; John 14:6.)
2. How does Matthew 6:19–24 reinforce the message of Proverbs 2?

TO THINK ABOUT AND DISCUSS

1. What are you doing to gain wisdom (see vv. 1–4)? List at least three ways you can deepen your quest for wisdom.
2. What benefits can you expect from your pursuit of wisdom (see vv. 5–11)? How does wisdom help you at home, in the workplace, and in relationships?
3. How does wisdom protect you from dangerous people (see vv. 12–22)?
4. Who are some of the dangerous men and women whom you must avoid?

4 A crash course in success

(3:1–35)

Proverbs 1 showed us the importance of seeking wisdom. Proverbs 2 instructed us in how to pursue wisdom and began to enumerate some of the benefits of wisdom. Proverbs 3 opens up the treasure house of wisdom. Waltke states, 'This chapter will give you a finer education than you could receive from most colleges and universities.'[6] And, I would add, at a much cheaper price!

The complete exposition of this chapter could fill a book. My objective is not to be comprehensive but rather to give an overview so that you might embark on a lifelong quest to dig deeper in seeking wisdom for yourself. The overarching theme of this chapter is that as you act wisely towards God and men, you will be successful in life.

Pay attention (vv. 1–4)

Again the father pleads with the son to remember and internalize what he is being taught (vv. 1,3). Forgetting parental instruction in wisdom is not merely a mental flaw but a moral evil (Deut. 8:11). We remember what is most important to us. For example, the son who often forgets his homework never forgets his soccer game. The father's law is not merely to be remembered intellectually but is to be faithfully kept (v. 1*a*). The wise father portrays wisdom and lovingkindness (covenant loyalty to God) as bound around one's neck or written on the tablet of the heart (v. 3). The father reminds the son of the great benefits of wisdom (vv. 2,4). Wisdom will add both to the quantity and quality of your years (v. 2). Verse 4 summarizes the rest of the chapter. Wisdom will bring you favour and a good reputation before both God and men.

Four ways to act wisely towards God (vv. 5–12)

Our author summarizes our duty to God in four commands. With each, he also expounds upon the blessing that directly results from obedience.

Trust in the LORD (vv. 5–6)

Trust God *entirely*, 'with all your heart' (v. 5*a*). God demands an undivided commitment to himself. Too often Israel had a loyalty divided between the LORD and the false gods of the nations. We can be tempted to trust the wisdom of the world rather than rely upon divine revelation. The psalmist says, 'I hate those who are double-minded' (Ps.

119:113). Jesus said, 'No one can serve two masters' (Matt. 6:24*a*), and he taught that the greatest commandment is to 'love the LORD your God with all your heart, and with all your soul, and with all your mind, and with all your strength' (Mark 12:30).

Trust God *exclusively*, and 'do not lean on your own understanding' (v. 5*b*). By nature we are inclined to foolishly rely upon our own inclinations and desires: 'All of us like sheep have gone astray, each of us has turned to his own way' (Isa. 53:6). Many people make crucial life decisions in areas such as marriage, finances, and vocation not based upon God's revealed Word but their feelings. Proverbs tells us that our feelings are unreliable: 'There is a way which seems right to a man, but its end is the way of death' (14:12); 'he who trusts in his own heart is a fool' (28:26*a*). A man may *feel* that he would be happier if he were to divorce his wife. A mother may not *feel* like using the rod of discipline on her children. In their quest to grow, churches may be tempted to resort to worldly methodologies that compromise biblical principles. The wise man does not lean on his own understanding but trusts that God's way is best. The one who chooses his own way arrogantly claims that he knows better than God.

The one who chooses his own way arrogantly claims that he knows better than God.

Proverbs also warns us against being improperly influenced by other people: 'The fear of man brings a snare, but he who trusts in the LORD will be exalted' (29:25). We must evaluate the counsel and influence of friends, family members, and worldly experts against the Word of God, and we must have the courage to risk their disapproval when Scripture directs us otherwise. The command to trust God also brings to mind the way of salvation. Conversion takes place when we repent of trusting in our own goodness and wisdom and put our faith in what God has done for us in Christ (Eph. 2:8–9).

Trust God *extensively*: 'In all your ways acknowledge Him' (v. 6*a*). We are not merely to acknowledge God's lordship over our religious life; we are to bring God's truth to bear on every aspect of life. We trust him in how we run our families, our education, our careers, our finances, and our friendships. He is Lord of all! Abraham Kuyper said, 'In the total expanse of human life there is not a single square inch of which the Christ, who alone is sovereign, does not declare, "That is mine!"'[7] The wise person is characterized by continuous contemplation of God and a ready observance of his will, not only in the great issues of life but also in day-to-day routine. No matter is too small for God's attention. To paraphrase one commentator, it is self-idolatry to think we can carry on even the most ordinary matters without his counsel.[8]

God blesses those who trust him: 'He will make your paths straight' (v. 6*b*). The person who trusts God entirely, exclusively, and extensively will enjoy success in life.

Fear the LORD (vv. 7–8)

The opposite of fearing the LORD is to 'be wise in your own eyes'. Those who fear God are humble. They realize that their own reasoning is tainted by sin: they have been wrong before, and they will probably be wrong again. Therefore, they are eager to gain wisdom from God so that they won't keep falling on their faces. Modern education is failing because it encourages students to be wise in their own eyes. It excludes God, who is the source of all truth, and teaches students to look solely to man for knowledge.

Many religious people are also wise in their own eyes (26:12). Certain scholars and 'experts' dare to sit in judgement on God's Word, criticizing and correcting Holy Scripture. Many professing Christians want to be influential but are not teachable. Even children can tune out their parents and teachers because they think they have already heard all the stories.

The one who fears the LORD will also 'turn away from evil' (v. 7*b*). The God-fearing man or woman realizes that because the LORD is the just, all-knowing, all-powerful, all-wise governor of the universe, no one ever benefits from going against his ways. The proud have no fear of God and therefore engage in all kinds of wickedness. They think they can fight God and win. The wise person is always conscious of God and is repulsed by evil, not merely because of a fear of the consequences but also because of a conviction that God's ways are the ways of greatest blessing. 'It will be healing to your body and refreshment to your bones' (v. 8).

Honour the LORD from your wealth (vv. 9–10)

For many of us there is no greater test of our love for and faith in God than how we spend our money. We give to the LORD's work, not because he needs our help, but to honour and worship him. The word translated 'honour' (v. 9) literally means 'heavy'. Such giving shows how highly you value God or how weighty you consider him to be. Giving is also an act of gratitude towards God who has given us all things (Deut. 8:18). Giving is an act of faith. When you give generously, you are expressing confidence that God will meet your needs and that you won't regret your charity.

You are to give the LORD 'the first of all your produce' (also translated 'firstfruits'). When the harvest arrived, the farmer was to give God the first and the best (Exod. 23:19). In modern terms, it means to pay God as soon as you receive your pay packet rather than waiting to see what is left over. You should give in proportion to how God has prospered you (1 Cor. 16:2).

> Fools think that giving to the Lord's work will make them poor. But God honours those who honour him.

The result of your generosity will be greater blessing (v. 10). Fools think that giving to the LORD's work will make them poor. But God honours those who honour him (1 Sam. 2:30). This does not necessarily mean that the godly will always abound in material riches, but we can be sure that he will meet our needs (Matt. 6:33) and that we are storing up treasure in heaven (Matt. 6:20).

It is also important to give wisely. Many religious organizations clamour for our money. Some make spectacular (and false) promises of worldly prosperity and health for their donors. Some who seek our charity are poor because of their laziness and should not be helped (10:4*a*; 2 Thes. 3:10). When you give foolishly, you are not giving to God.

Embrace the LORD's discipline (vv. 11–12)

The path of life is not always smooth and easy for God's people. While verses 9–10 tell us how to honour God during prosperity, verses 11–12 train us to honour God in the midst of adversity.

Why does God discipline us? The word 'discipline' in verse 11 is also translated 'instruction' in other places (1:2) and is also used of parental discipline (13:24). God is our Father who is training us for maturity. Because Christ has already removed our guilt (2 Cor. 5:21), our suffering is not punitive, but corrective. Some lessons can only be learned through hardship and suffering. Even our Lord Jesus 'learned obedience from the things which he suffered' (Heb. 5:8). His suffering proves that not all suffering is due to personal sin. Nor does your pain mean that you are out of God's favour. Instead, suffering proves your sonship. God is so committed to our good that he is willing to bring suffering into our lives so we might gain wisdom and good character. He is like the soccer coach who makes the players run drills until they are ready to collapse in exhaustion. While the players may not enjoy their training, they will be thankful when the big game comes. 'All discipline for the moment seems not to be joyful, but sorrowful; yet to those who have been trained by it, afterwards it yields the peaceful fruit of righteousness' (Heb. 12:11). If you are having trouble in a particular area such as your finances, you might consider whether there are lessons God is teaching you, such as to avoid debt.

Just as some children foolishly resist parental discipline,

we are warned not to 'reject the discipline of the LORD, or loathe his reproof' (v. 11). Some professing Christians become bitter and even angry with God when they endure physical and emotional pain. Others are tempted to despair, wallowing in their misery. Instead, we should remember that we are children in whom our heavenly Father delights (v. 12*b*) and that he is sovereignly allowing us to suffer because he loves us (13:24). Thank God that he cares enough about us to discipline us as a father and doesn't let us get away with much for long. Unlike that of our earthly fathers, God's discipline is perfect (Heb. 12:9–10), which means that you can be sure that every trial that comes into your life is perfectly designed by your heavenly Father for your benefit. It has been said, 'He will melt you in his furnace that he may stamp you with his image.' The psalmist states, 'Before I was afflicted I went astray, but now I keep your word' (Ps. 119:67).

Three ways to act wisely towards men (vv. 27–35)

Repay your needy neighbour (vv. 27–28)

The law demanded that the labourer be paid his wages daily before the sun set, 'so that he will not cry against you to the LORD and it become sin in you' (Deut. 24:15). Employers sometimes take advantage of those who are weak. When we lived in Saudi Arabia, we met many labourers from developing countries whose employers treated them as virtual slaves, cruelly refusing to give them the pay and benefits that had been promised.

The principle of timely payment also applies to those to

whom we owe debts. 'The wicked borrows and does not pay back' (Ps. 37:21*a*). Evil men put off their creditors, make excuses, and try to avoid their obligations. This applies to financial debts (such as not paying your share of a restaurant tab) or borrowed items (books from your friend's library, for example). Unnecessary delays and excuses are unacceptable. A wise man is burdened by his debts and relieves himself of his obligations at the first possible opportunity.

The Bible extends this principle even further, instructing us to 'owe nothing to anyone except to love one another' (Rom. 13:8*a*). The law put God's people under obligation to help the widow and the orphan. Jesus tells the story of the Good Samaritan that illustrates our duty to care for those in need. Paul also acknowledges that those of us who have the gospel have a spiritual debt to all men to share the good news. 'I am under obligation both to Greeks and to barbarians, both to the wise and the foolish' (Rom. 1:14).

The standards of Scripture go beyond cut-throat capitalism.

Do not harm your innocent neighbour (vv. 29–30)

People who live together in a community need to be able to trust one another. We ought to be careful to pursue the good of our neighbours. Don't slander them with gossip (20:19). Don't cheat or take advantage of them financially (20:10,14). Evil men live by the laws of the economic jungle and prey on the naive and weak. The standards of Scripture go beyond cut-throat capitalism. It is unacceptable for one who fears the LORD to take advantage of the weak by charging an inflated price or hiding product defects. Nor should we contend with others needlessly (v. 30). The New Testament forbids one believer from suing another in the courts (1 Cor. 6:1–8). Those who are wise are not obsessed with their rights but rather seek to imitate Jesus, who did not insist upon his prerogatives (Phil. 2:3–8; 1 Peter 2:21–24) and did good to his enemies.

Do not envy your wicked neighbour (vv. 31–35)

In the short term, it can appear that evil and violent men get ahead. Perverse politicians and wicked celebrities seem to mock God with impunity while enjoying the best the world has to offer. You can be tempted to envy their prosperity (Ps. 73:3) and question whether it pays to be good and wise. You may wonder why God allows so much evil in the world. In the long run, however, their crimes do not pay (Ps. 73:17). Their sins offend the LORD who knows all things (Prov. 3:32). Their prosperity will be short-lived. He will judge them. The wicked will become a spectacle of shame (v. 35*b*) because 'God is opposed to the proud, but gives grace to the humble' (James 4:6).

If you act wisely towards God and men, you will enjoy success (vv. 2,4,13–26,32–35)

Throughout this entire chapter, there have been numerous promises of blessings attached to the appeal of wisdom. These blessings include:

- You will enjoy a long, healthy and pleasant life (vv. 2,6,8,16*a*,17–18). Our author portrays wisdom as the tree of life (v. 18), access to which Adam lost in the Fall but

Jesus regained by his completed work (Gen. 2:9; Rev. 22:2).

- You will enjoy the favour of God and men (vv. 4,35*a*).
- You will enjoy material prosperity (vv. 10,16*b*).
- You will be enriched with spiritual treasures (vv. 14–15).
- You will partake of the same wisdom by which God created the world (vv. 19–20). Proverbs 8 develops this concept in greater detail.
- You will be protected from trouble and fear (vv. 22–26). You will sleep soundly because you have no earthly fears (v. 24). God is your security and confidence.
- You will be privy to the intimate counsels (secrets) of God who 'is intimate with the upright' (v. 32*b*).
- You will be honoured by God (v. 35*a*).

Does Proverbs promise too much?

The wise do not always enjoy material wealth and long life. Some Christians die young through cancer or a car accident. Some believers lose their jobs and endure poverty. As explained earlier, Proverbs contains maxims that describe the way life generally works in God's world. While those who follow God's commands generally enjoy long life and prosperity, this is not an absolute promise to every individual, especially in the short term. God in his sovereign wisdom may allow us to suffer for his glory (Rom. 8:28). Waltke says, 'If God rewarded virtue immediately, the son would confound pleasure with piety, using piety and ethics to satisfy his prurient interests'[9] rather than living by faith.

Furthermore, the book of Proverbs was written under the Old Covenant, in which physical blessings and curses were directly tied to covenant faithfulness for the nation of Israel (see Lev. 26; Deut. 28). Because we live under the New Covenant, there is no longer a theocratic political kingdom with covenant blessings and curses.

The kingdom blessings and curses in Proverbs do look ahead to the ultimate eschatological (end times) blessings that will be enjoyed by the righteous and the curses that will fall upon the wicked in God's eternal kingdom (v. 33–35; 2:21–22) at Christ's return (Rev. 22:14). In the end, the meek will inherit the earth and the evildoers will be condemned (Ps. 37:29; Matt. 5:5; Rev. 22:14). One day we will enjoy heavenly treasure and partake of the tree of life (Prov. 3:14–15,18), but in the meantime, the wise trust God and endure (vv. 5–6).

Conclusion

If you are honest with yourself, you may realize that you have not pursued wisdom as you should. Apart from God's grace, we would all be excluded from the blessings of wisdom. Jesus has come to give us wisdom and life. He lived a life of perfect wisdom towards both God and men. He endured the curse (v. 33) of the punishment and dishonour we deserved because of our sinful folly. Our chastisement fell upon him (Isa. 53:5; 1 Peter 3:18). Now through him we have been made wise unto salvation. We are partakers of the tree of life (Prov. 3:18). Stop trusting in yourself, and trust him alone.

FOR FURTHER STUDY

1. Trace the theme of the tree of life through the Bible, and draw some conclusions about the significance of the reference to it in Proverbs 3:18. (See Gen. 2:9; Jer. 17:7–8; Rev. 22:2.)
2. In what sense did the curses of foolishness and wickedness fall upon Christ? (See Prov. 3:33; Gal. 3:13.)

TO THINK ABOUT AND DISCUSS

1. Evaluate yourself according to the four ways in which we should act wisely towards God (3:5–12). In which areas would you like to see growth?
2. Evaluate yourself in light of the three ways in which we should act wisely towards men (3:27–35). Can you think of a neighbour with whom you need to act wisely in a particular situation?
3. In what sense are the blessings of wisdom conditional? In what sense are the blessings unconditional? Which earthly blessings have you enjoyed from wise living? What consequences have you suffered from folly?
4. When has God corrected you through discipline? Are you willing to give him thanks?
5. What do you owe to others? What plans have you made to pay your debts (material and spiritual)?

5 Sexual wisdom

(5:1–23; 6:20–35; 7:1–27)

There is no topic in Proverbs to which more emphasis is given than that of sexual purity. The irony is great in light of the fact that Solomon was virtually ruined because of his attraction to foreign wives (1 Kings 11).

Times do not change. We live in an age in which sexual immorality is on display virtually everywhere. Sadly, sexual sin continues to have a devastating impact on the church. Scandals among her leaders have besmirched the reputation of Christ in the world. Families have been torn apart by sexual immorality.

Proverbs speaks of moral purity in both symbolic and literal terms. On the symbolic level, the young man is encouraged to make Lady Wisdom his true bride and is warned to resist the seductions of Madame Folly, who symbolizes the temptation to unfaithfulness towards God

(James 4:4). In chapters 8–9, Lady Wisdom and Madame Folly invite the young man to their banquets, and he must choose where he will dine. Proverbs also talks about the blessings of a (literal) godly wife (18:22; 31:10–31) and warns the young man against the wiles of the adulteress. The literal and the symbolic portrayals are woven together and support each other.

Sex education takes place in the home (5:1–4; 6:20–24; 7:1–5)

Each of the three discourses about adultery comes from the lips of a father to his beloved son. This reminds us of the duty of parents to teach their children about the sexual facts of life. They should proclaim the right use of God's gift of sex as a joyous expression of marital union, the fruit of which is children. They should also warn of the severe consequences of the abuse of God's gift of sex. We live in a dangerous world and should not pull any punches as we prepare our children for the temptations they will face. They need to be aware of the wiles of the seductress (heterosexual or homosexual). They need specific instruction on what to do when they are tempted. Naive children are vulnerable children.

We live in a dangerous world and should not pull any punches as we prepare our children for the temptations they will face.

Parents who abdicate this duty to the schools, to peers, and to the entertainment industry are contributing to the ruin of their children. The world promotes sinful folly.

Young people are not to be left to follow their own feelings in this area. They need parental oversight and direction.

Wisdom offers a true sex education that will protect you from the world and equip you to enjoy a pure, joyful, and satisfying life. She identifies one woman (the adulteress) who can destroy you and two women (Lady Wisdom and a good wife) who will protect you, even saving your life.

It is not just young people who need this exhortation. Remember that King David fell into adultery in midlife (2 Sam. 11).

The adulteress can destroy you (7:6–23)

Proverbs 7 dramatically describes the seduction of a naive young man. In contrast to portrayals of such events in film and television, Scripture vividly describes sin without making it attractive. The writer describes a scene he sees outside his window. Such a scene could have taken place 3,000 years ago or yesterday.

The prey (vv. 6–9)

The seduction reads like a nature film in which the lion stalks an unsuspecting zebra that has become separated from the herd. The victim is not a hardened sinner, but he is 'naive' (v. 7). He doesn't fully understand what is about to happen to him. This feather-brained man, however, is culpable. He hasn't heeded the parental warnings of wisdom. He walks right into temptation ('near her corner', v. 8), even though he has been told not to go near her door (5:8). Perhaps he is curious about the disreputable area of town about which he has heard. He has heard about certain movies, websites, or bars but has never personally experienced them. Perhaps he thinks himself wise to the ways of the world and able to resist (but see 1 Cor. 10:12). Perhaps he, like David, has time on his hands because of sinful idleness (2 Sam. 11:1). Perhaps he assumes that he will be anonymous because of the darkness of night (v. 9), not realizing that darkness is a time of evil and danger (4:19; John 3:19).

The huntress and her tactics (vv. 10–20)

She besieges every sense (vv. 10–17)

In John Bunyan's allegory *The Holy War*, the city of Mansoul is attacked at various gates: the Ear-gate, the Eye-gate, the Nose-gate, etc. So the adulteress attacks the Eye-gate, seeking to entice by her alluring appearance (v. 10*b*; 6:25*b*). Her clothes reveal her perfectly proportioned body. Her eyelids seek to capture the young man's attention. She assaults the Ear-gate with her flattering words (vv. 5,15,21; 5:3; 6:24*b*). Her tongue is smooth. She knows how to capture a man's heart through flattery. She will stroke his ego in a way no one else ever has. 'You are so strong, so smart, and so good. You are just the man for whom I have been waiting' (see v. 15). Incredibly, the naive youth believes her. She attacks the Feel-gate with her touch (v. 13). Her lips are warm. Her skin is soft. He cannot resist. Her perfume wafts through the Smell-gate (vv. 16–17). She even attacks the Mouth-gate, knowing that the way to a man's heart is his stomach (v. 14).

This is also an implicit reminder to ladies not to become seductresses, even inadvertently, by the way you dress and act. A naive woman follows the fashions of the world and becomes a stumbling block to her brothers. Then, in her ignorance, she can't understand why men seek her attention for all the wrong reasons.

She lures you with promises of the ultimate in sensual exhilaration (vv. 16,18)

She sounds like the contemporary pop songs encouraging you to cast off your inhibitions and make love until the sun rises (v. 18).

She overcomes your doubts and fears (vv. 19–20)

She overcomes every objection. 'We won't get caught. My husband [or father] has left town and will be gone a long time.' 'We're consenting adults. No one has to know.' 'What happens in Vegas stays in Vegas!' 'You deserve what your spouse doesn't give you. Your marriage is as good as over anyway.' 'It is all right if we have sex because some day we will be married.' 'We'll practise safe sex.' She even portrays herself as religious (v. 14): 'God made us this way. We can't help ourselves.' 'We can do penance in the morning. God will forgive us.'

The kill (vv. 21–23)

The naive young victim is overwhelmed. His defences are broken down. Her trap closes and it is too late for him to escape. He is like the dumb ox who thinks he is going to pasture but really is going to slaughter (vv. 22–23). The seductress has many victims (v. 26), even among those who are supposed to be leaders and examples among God's people.

With this description, the father is hoping to train his son to recognize the adulteress and to flee (2 Tim. 2:22). In addition to teaching him to avoid the adulteress, he also encourages his son to embrace two women, one symbolic and the other literal.

Make Wisdom your first love (4:5–9; 7:4–5)

The father describes Wisdom as the perfect lover. She is better than a wife. A wife alone without Wisdom will not be enough to keep you free from sin. You may not always have a wife nearby. Some wives are not helpful in overcoming temptation (21:9), but Wisdom protects every man who seeks her from sexual impurity. No man who falls into sexual sin can blame his singleness or a bad wife, because Wisdom alone would have protected him if he had sought her. The love of Wisdom is the love of God (Mark 12:30). Wisdom teaches you not to live for worldly pleasure (2 Tim. 3:4) but rather to find perfect satisfaction in the LORD (9:1–5; Isa. 55:1–2; 12:2; 44:3). Wisdom will exalt you (4:8) like a good wife who is a crown to her husband (12:4).

Lady Wisdom will deliver you from immorality

Wisdom will enable you to repulse the attacks and to avoid the snares of the adulteress. She will strengthen and guard the gates of your soul.

Lady Wisdom helps you see the true nature of the seductress

In contrast to worldly entertainment, which usually portrays loose women sympathetically, Wisdom shows the bad character of the seductress. She is cunning and deceitful

(7:10). Her flattery spreads a net in which the young man will be trapped (29:5). She feigns fidelity to her lovers, yet she truly loves no one. She is boisterous and hardened (7:11*a*). She has no fear of God. Her conscience has been singed. 'This is the way of an adulterous woman: She eats and wipes her mouth, and says "I have done no wrong"' (30:20). She is brazen and shameless (7:13). She is rebellious and is unwilling to commit to a husband, to children, and to a home (7:11*b*–12; 2:17). You think you are using her, but in reality she is the one who is using you. She is a religious hypocrite (7:14). She is a counterfeit wife offering counterfeit love (7:18). It is a travesty to call what she gives 'love'. Matthew Henry states, 'It is a pity that the name of love should be thus abused.'[10] Sexual union has been designed by God as an expression of covenant commitment and self-sacrificing love. What the adulteress offers is brutish and fleeting.

Lady Wisdom shows you why sexual immorality is wrong

Sexual immorality is first and foremost a sin against God (Ps. 51:5; James 4:4; Gen. 39:9), thereby violating the greatest commandment to love him with all your heart. Sexual sin is also a violation of the second greatest commandment, of the love you should have for your neighbour (6:29; Lev. 19:16–18; Exod. 20:14). Through immorality you steal from and harm the innocent spouse(s) and other family members. You also bring God's judgement upon your partner in adultery.

Lady Wisdom reminds you of the deadly consequences of immorality (5:4–5,11–12,22–23; 6:26–35; 7:22–27)

That which seems to begin with sweetness and pleasure has a

bitter end. In contrast to worldly entertainment, which focuses upon the immediate sensual pleasures of sexual immorality, Proverbs extensively portrays the life-destroying results of sin.

Sexual sin will affect you physically (5:9,11; 6:34–35)

Your energy will be sapped through guilt (Ps. 32:3–4). The aggrieved spouse may seek revenge, perhaps taking your life (6:34–35). Sexually transmitted diseases appear to be another God-ordained consequence of immorality.

Sexual sin will ruin you financially (5:10; 6:26a,30–31; 29:3)

Immorality is expensive. The adulteress takes financial advantage of her victims. I have counselled men who have squandered small fortunes on food, gifts, and hotels. Others have been blackmailed by scorned lovers who threatened to reveal the truth to the innocent spouses. Many have squandered large sums through cybersex and phone sex. Few experiences in life are more expensive than divorce, which is often the result of immorality.

Sexual sin will destroy your reputation (5:14; 6:33)

The good name that you have spent a lifetime protecting can be lost in one night. While our culture as a whole often embraces immorality, the community of the righteous upholds God's standards.

Sexual sin will break apart your family (5:16–17)

You will lose the trust and respect of your spouse and children. You may wind up divorced and alone. You may father illegitimate children, depriving them of the blessings of being raised by a mother and father in a God-fearing home. You may infect your wife with a sexually transmitted disease.

Your sin will find you out (6:27–29; Num. 32:23)

Madame Folly, like the serpent in Genesis 3, promises that you will not die. Perhaps you begin by dabbling with sin. You fear lightning will fall from the sky; but when it does not, you become more brazen. You are playing with fire (6:27). It is just a matter of time before your judgement comes. Ultimately you will be hit, not by Cupid's arrow, but by God's arrow of judgement (7:22–23,26–27).

Lady Wisdom trains you to stay far away from sexual temptation

She teaches you to guard your heart (4:23; 7:3,25). She warns you not to even desire what is not yours (Matt. 5:27–28; Exod. 20:17). Lust in the heart gives birth to sin, resulting in death (James 1:14–15). Take responsibility for what you allow to enter your Eye- and Ear-gates. Take radical action to avoid temptation (Matt. 5:29; 2 Tim. 2:22). Wisdom exhorts you to stay as far away as possible from sexual sin (5:8). I have heard it said, 'Those who fall into immorality usually don't fall far.' Set standards for your relationships with the opposite sex and the entertainment to which you expose yourself. Don't be naive, thinking that you could never fall sexually. 'Let him who thinks he stands take heed that he does not fall' (1 Cor. 10:12).

Your wife can also protect you from immorality (5:15–23)

Proverbs does not show merely the sordid side of sex; it also shows the beauty and exhilaration of marital love.

Find sexual happiness with your spouse (5:15–17)

The answer to sexual desire is not mere abstinence but marital delight. Sex itself is not evil but rather is a gift of God when enjoyed by two people who have entered into the covenant of marriage. The New Testament also teaches that marriage, including the sexual union, is honourable before God (Heb. 13:4). This is in stark opposition to some in Christendom who have taught that sexual desire is inherently evil and that those who want to serve God in significant ways must be celibate. The apostle Paul warned that false teachers would arise who would 'forbid marriage' (1 Tim. 4:3). Scandals throughout church history and in recent years demonstrate that efforts to suppress human sexuality often result in secret and wicked sexual expression. One of the great advances of the Reformation was the recovery of consistent biblical teaching on the wholesomeness of marriage, including the marriage bed (Eccles. 9:9).

Sex within marriage has been given by God to help both the husband and the wife to fulfil sexual desire.

Sex within marriage has been given by God to help both the husband and the wife to fulfil sexual desire. Paul tells those who are single that it is better to marry than to burn with sexual desire (1 Cor. 7:9). He also exhorts husbands and wives to fulfil their marital duties to each other so that they will not be tempted to sin (1 Cor. 7:3–5). Some married couples fail to fulfil this duty to each other because of selfishness or perhaps because one or both spouses have an unbiblical view of sex as being merely a necessary evil for procreation. Husbands and wives should not focus upon their own wants and desires (or lack of desire) but must selflessly give themselves to each other sexually as an expression of love and commitment.

A man is to drink exclusively from his 'own cistern' (5:15), which means that all of a man's sexual energy is to be directed to his wife. She is his exclusive source of sexual refreshment. Negatively, he is not to disperse his sexual energy outside his marriage (vv. 16–17). Any sexual act or thought which is not directed towards his wife is sinful and destructive. This truth is reinforced by our Lord Jesus, who makes it clear that even looking at or thinking (fantasizing) about someone other than your wife is adultery (Matt. 5:27–28). Paul tells men that their bodies, including their minds and eyes, belong exclusively to their wives for their joy (1 Cor. 7:3–4). This is why solo sex is wrong. Your body is not your own, and sex isn't primarily about pleasing yourself. Sex is meant to be relational, an expression of love to bring happiness to your spouse.

The exclusivity of sex within marriage also implies that sex is a private matter. The Song of Solomon speaks of marital love as a garden (S. of S. 4:12–15; 5:1) for the exclusive enjoyment of the married lovers. It is wrong to violate the privacy of marital love through immodesty or voyeurism.

Marital sex is exhilarating (5:18–19)

The greatest possible sexual happiness is to be found with your wife, not with a strange woman. A husband and his wife should fully enjoy pleasures which thrill all of their senses. The Song of Solomon describes how the man and his bride are thrilled by the sights, the sounds, the smells, the touches, and the tastes of marital love (S. of S. 1:2–3; 2:3,6,14; 4:9,14; 5:1). Within the garden of marital love, all five sense gates can be opened wide for mutual enjoyment. You can let yourself go with your spouse. Waltke speaks of this text's 'biblical eroticism of male virility and female sexual beauty and charm'.[11] Husband and wife can forget the cares of life, legitimately enjoying being 'intoxicated' (another possible translation of 'exhilarated' in 5:19*c*) with their love for each other. The man who has to look away from all the other female breasts put on display in our culture can freely enjoy his wife's breasts (5:19*b*). The wife may delight in being desired and being overwhelmed by the love of her husband. Their sexual thirst can be quenched in a way that pleases God.

Husband and wife can forget the cares of life, legitimately enjoying being 'intoxicated' … with their love for each other.

Practise 'safe sex' (5:20–23)

Safe sex is sex with your spouse. If you are sexually exhilarated with your wife, the harlot's seductions won't affect you. Why would anyone who is fully enjoying the blessings of marriage be so foolish as to ruin everything by going to a strange woman who will ruin his life?

Some caveats

This beautiful portrayal of marital joy assumes a godly marriage. Sexual union is meant to be an expression of love between a husband and a wife who are committed to each other and to God. As both fulfil their God-given roles in marriage and sacrificially care for each other, the sexual union takes place naturally and joyfully. The selfish man who treats his wife badly all day should not be surprised when his evenings don't fully meet his hopes and expectations. If you are married, tend your (sexual) garden. Spend time together promoting personal intimacy. Take care of yourself physically. Pull up the weeds of unresolved conflict and sinful patterns of communication. Don't take each other for granted but cultivate romance.

If you are single, protect and preserve your garden. Your sexuality belongs to your future spouse. Keep it locked until the day of your wedding, when you and your spouse can enter and enjoy God's gifts without shame or regret.

As wonderful as married love can be, Wisdom must still be your first love. If you are not wise, a wife will not deliver you from sexual temptation.

Summary

Proverbs 5–7 tells us about three women. The adulteress can kill you. Wisdom will save you. Your wife can help you.

Conclusion: Christ is our true love

Probably none of us is without sin in the area of moral purity. We have all, at times, been unfaithful and unwise. On a spiritual level, we have all been guilty of loving the world too much (1 John 2:15), which is unfaithfulness to God. Because God is a holy and jealous God, we deserve his wrath.

Thank God for the Lord Jesus, who cleanses us from our sin and makes us wise. Though we prostituted ourselves with the world, he has bought us with his blood and cleansed us by his grace. He purifies and transforms us (1 Cor. 6:9–11; 2 Cor. 5:17). He quenches our spiritual thirst and provides the ultimate satisfaction for our souls (Prov. 14:27; Isa. 12:3; Zech. 13:1; John 4:14). He rejoices over us just as a bridegroom rejoices over his bride (Isa. 62:5). Make him your first love!

FOR FURTHER STUDY

1. Compare and contrast the sensual appeal of the adulteress (Proverbs 7) with the sensual delights described in the Song of Solomon.
2. How does the teaching of Proverbs about sexual purity and marriage compare with the teachings of Paul (1 Cor. 7) and Jesus (Matt. 5:27–30)?

TO THINK ABOUT AND DISCUSS

1. What is the role of the family in sex education? How should parents go about teaching their children about sex (see 5:1; 6:20; 7:1)?
2. How can Wisdom protect you from sexual immorality?
3. What particular changes can you make in your life to win the fight for purity?
4. How can a spouse help guard you from sexual sin?
5. Why is Wisdom more important than a husband or wife?
6. Contrast the way in which the Bible speaks about human sexuality with the way in which sexual matters are portrayed in worldly media.

6 The call of Wisdom and the call of Christ

(8:1–9:18)

After extensive warnings about the seductions of the immoral woman in chapters 5–7, Lady Wisdom is given a final opportunity to show off her beauty in chapters 8–9.

This is a fitting climax to the first nine chapters of Proverbs, which are an extended appeal for the young person to devote his or her life to pursuing Wisdom, the personification of the soul's true love.

Bruce Waltke points out seven areas of contrast between Lady Wisdom and the seductress.[12]

- The adulteress calls the young man from the darkness and in secret (7:9); Wisdom's call is open and public (8:1–3).
- The wayward woman is sexually loose (7:10); Wisdom is holy (8:8*a*).
- The wayward woman is an unreliable liar (7:11); Wisdom is truthful and faithful (8:8*b*–9).

- The seductress gives you her body but not herself (2:17); Wisdom offers you true love (8:17).
- The adulteress offers fleeting pleasures; Wisdom provides everlasting joy (8:18).
- The adulteress is selfish, giving only to get; Wisdom delights to give and serve.
- The seductress leads you to a chamber of death (7:27); Wisdom gives you everlasting life (8:35; 3:18).

Who is Wisdom?

Wisdom is personified as a woman in Proverbs. Wisdom is an attribute of God (Job 12:13; Eph. 1:8; Jer. 10:12) that he shares with those who are faithful to his covenant. The wisdom of God is revealed in Scripture (Ps. 19:7–11).

Jesus Christ is wisdom incarnate

Isaiah 11:2 says of the Messiah, 'The Spirit of the LORD will rest on Him, the spirit of wisdom and understanding, the spirit of counsel and strength, the spirit of knowledge and the fear of the LORD.' 1 Corinthians 1:30 tells us that he 'became to us wisdom from God'. Waltke writes, 'She [wisdom] emerges as a unique personality whose only peer is Jesus Christ.'[13] The book of Proverbs, like all Scripture, points to Christ (see Luke 24:44–47). The emphasis of this chapter is to show that when Proverbs speaks of wisdom, Proverbs is speaking of Christ.

Wisdom and Jesus call out to you (8:1–5)

Wisdom is portrayed as going through the city, loudly pleading with the naive to heed her call (vv. 1–4; see also

1:20–21). Jesus also pleaded with sinners: 'Come to Me, all who are weary and heavy-laden, and I will give you rest. Take My yoke upon you and learn from Me, for I am gentle and humble in heart, and you will find rest for your souls. For My yoke is easy and My burden is light' (Matt. 11:28–30). Wisdom calls out to all classes of people indiscriminately (vv. 4–5; see also 1:22). Though she is great, she condescends to reach out to the naive and lowly (v. 5). Jesus, who is King of kings, condescends to seek out sinful humanity as he freely offers himself to all. 'Jesus stood and cried out, saying, "If anyone is thirsty, let him come to Me and drink. He who believes in Me, as the Scripture said, 'From his innermost being will flow rivers of living water'"' (John 7:37–38). Like Wisdom, Jesus sends his servants out into the world to plead with sinners to believe (9:3; Luke 14:23; Matt. 28:18–20).

Wisdom reveals herself only to those who have spiritual understanding.

Wisdom and Jesus should be treasured (8:6–11)

The teaching of Wisdom is both excellent and righteous (vv. 6–8). There is nothing false or crooked in her teaching. Christ is 'the power of God and the wisdom of God' (1 Cor. 1:24). In him there is no sin or waywardness (2 Cor. 5:21; Heb. 4:15). He is truth incarnate (John 14:6). Wisdom is not discovered by the proud. Nor is wisdom gained through mere human reason. Wisdom reveals herself only to those who have spiritual understanding. You must have a heart that is humble like that of a child (Matt. 18:4) and receptive to spiritual knowledge if you are to receive wisdom from Christ (1 Cor. 2:14; 1:18–25; Matt. 11:25). Wisdom is the most precious thing (vv. 10–11). If you pursue any other goal in life—money, pleasure, or fame—wisdom will elude you. If you lack wisdom, it is because you haven't valued it as highly as you should have. The wisdom contained in Scripture is better than gold (Ps. 119:14,72,127). Jesus is our greatest treasure, the one 'in whom are hidden all the treasures of wisdom and knowledge' (Col. 2:3). He is the pearl of great value and the treasure hidden in the field (Matt. 13:44–46). You must fully commit yourself to Wisdom and to Christ. You cannot have Wisdom as your bride while keeping Folly as your mistress.

Wisdom and Jesus teach you to humbly fear God (8:12–13)

Wisdom hides herself from those who are wise in their own eyes (3:7). Those who learn from her are humbled and hate evil. Jesus was meek and humble (Matt. 20:28; Phil. 2:5–8). He teaches his followers to emulate his humility (Matt. 20:25–27; Phil. 2:3–4) and promises that his 'gentle' (meek or humble) ones will inherit the earth (Matt. 5:5). God has, in Christ, chosen the humble to shame the worldly-wise and powerful (1 Cor. 1:26–29).

Wisdom and Jesus offer you success (8:14–16)

Under the Old Covenant, when kings ruled according to wisdom and justice they enjoyed great prosperity (1 Kings 3–10; 2 Kings 18). The best of the rulers of Israel and Judah were types of the Messiah who would rule with perfect wisdom and justice. King Jesus reigns with the wisdom taught by Proverbs. Jeremiah 23:5 states, 'I will raise up for David a righteous Branch; and He will reign as king and act wisely' (see also Isa. 11:1–5; 9:6–7). Jesus succeeds perfectly in his rule, crushing all his wicked foes (1 Cor. 15:25). 'He will reign forever and ever' (Rev. 11:15), and we shall reign with him (Rev. 22:5).

Wisdom and Jesus offer you great rewards (8:17–21)

Wisdom loves and blesses those who love and seek her (v. 17). They enjoy success in their vocations, in their families, with their finances, and in their relationships. Jesus loves and blesses those who seek him (John 14:21; Matt. 7:7–11). Because we are by nature wayward and would never seek him (Rom. 8:7–8), he draws us to himself, giving us new desire for wisdom (Jer. 31:3; Rom. 8:9–11; 1 John 4:19). Just as Wisdom offers great treasure to those who seek her, so Jesus makes all who come to him spiritually rich, at great cost to himself (2 Cor. 8:9; Matt. 6:19–20; Rev. 3:18). In him we have an imperishable heavenly inheritance (1 Peter 1:4–5).

Wisdom and Christ display their glory in creation (8:22–31)

There is probably no passage in Proverbs that more directly points to Christ than the description of the role of Wisdom in the creation. Wisdom is said to be from everlasting (vv. 22–23), just as Jesus is eternal and one with the Father (John 1:1–2; 17:5). The fact that Wisdom was 'brought forth' (vv. 24–26) reminds us of the eternal sonship of Christ (Col. 1:15; Ps. 2:12; John 3:16).[14] Wisdom was present at and mediated the glorious work of creation (vv. 27–30*a*). The New

Testament reveals God the Son to be the agent of creation: 'All things came into being through Him, and apart from Him nothing came into being that has come into being' (John 1:3; see also Col. 1:16; Heb. 1:2). The beauty of Wisdom and the beauty of Christ are displayed in the skies, the seas, and on the land. Wisdom delights in God's work of creation (vv. 30*c*–31*a*; Gen. 1:31). Jesus delights in the Father, always doing his will (Ps. 40:8; Heb. 10:7; John 4:34; 6:38) in his greater work of redemption. Just as God delighted in Wisdom at creation (v. 30*b*; Gen. 1:31), so the Father also delights in the Son's work of redemption (Isa. 42:1; Matt. 3:17; 17:5; Col. 1:3). Wisdom rejoices in mankind as the pinnacle of God's creation (v. 31*b*). Christ rejoices in the work of redeeming mankind (Heb. 12:2; Isa. 53:10–11), from which he gains the greatest satisfaction. Jesus' new creation, the church, manifests God's wisdom (Col. 1:18; Eph. 3:10).

If God himself required wisdom in order to execute the creation, how much more do we need wisdom to accomplish anything in our lives!

The role of Wisdom in the creation is also a practical reminder for us. If God himself required wisdom in order to execute the creation, how much more do we need wisdom to accomplish anything in our lives (family, vocation, relationships, ministry, etc.)! Jesus said, 'I am the vine, you are the branches; he who abides in Me and I in him, he bears much fruit, for apart from Me you can do nothing' (John 15:5).

Wisdom and Christ will bless you with life (8:32–36)

The man who heeds and earnestly seeks wisdom obtains life and favour from God (vv. 32–35). The one who comes to Christ in faith receives everlasting life (John 1:4; 5:24; 11:25; 14:6). Just as the person who turns from Wisdom brings destruction and death upon him- or herself (v. 36), so the one who rejects Christ will suffer everlasting death (John 3:18–19; 12:48).

Wisdom and Christ invite you to a feast (9:1–5)

There are actually two competing dinner invitations in Proverbs 9. Lady Wisdom calls the naive to turn away from Folly and to feast at her elegant table. Madame Folly has prepared a deadly banquet of stolen (illicit) foods that will poison the soul (9:15–18). The theme of spiritual food is developed elsewhere in the Old Testament, including Psalm 23, in which the LORD who is our Shepherd prepares a table for us. The psalmist also sings, 'How sweet are Your words to my taste! Yes, sweeter than honey to my mouth!' (Ps. 119:103). Isaiah 55:1–2 offers a very striking parallel to Proverbs 9 as God pleads through the prophet for us to stop wasting our money on food that does not satisfy (as is served at Madame Folly's table) but instead to eat the sumptuous fare he freely offers. Jesus extends this theme as he offers us living water to drink (John 4:10; 7:37–38). He even invites us to feed upon himself, saying,

> I am the bread of life. Your fathers ate the manna in the wilderness, and they died. This is the bread which comes down out of heaven, so that one may eat of it and not die. I am

> the living bread that came down out of heaven; if anyone eats of this bread, he will live forever; and the bread also which I will give for the life of the world is My flesh ... Truly, truly, I say to you, unless you eat the flesh of the Son of Man and drink His blood, you have no life in yourselves. He who eats My flesh and drinks My blood has eternal life, and I will raise him up on the last day. For My flesh is true food, and My blood is true drink (John 6:48–55).

Just as Wisdom has 'built her house' as your feasting place (9:1), so Jesus is building his house, the church (Matt. 16:18; 1 Tim. 3:15; Heb. 3:3–4; Eph. 2:20–22). The fellowship of the church is centred on the Lord's Supper, a feast of remembrance in which we feed upon Christ by faith. We look forward to an everlasting heavenly feast when he returns (Rev. 19:9).

What is your reply to Wisdom and to Jesus?

When one is invited to a formal dinner party, a reply is expected. What is your response to God's gracious invitation? Do you realize that by nature you are a foolish simpleton who desperately needs Wisdom? Do you hunger for truth? Will you commit yourself? Only those who humbly seek Wisdom will receive God's blessing.

Don't be a scoffer

It is significant that, while Wisdom invites the naive (simpleton) to her banquet, she doesn't bother asking the scoffer (9:7–8). The scoffer is proud and hardened beyond reproof. He mocks Wisdom (and Christ). If you join the scoffer in rejecting Wisdom, you will be to blame for your own doom (9:12*b*,18). Madame Folly is anti-wisdom and anti-Christ. Those who follow after her will die.

Hunger after God, and he will fill you

Say to yourself, 'I will devote myself to seeking Wisdom, which is Jesus Christ.'

> Thus says the LORD, 'Let not a wise man boast of his wisdom, and let not the mighty man boast of his might, let not a rich man boast of his riches; but let him who boasts boast of this, that he understands and knows Me, that I am the LORD who exercises lovingkindness, justice and righteousness on earth; for I delight in these things,' declares the LORD (Jer. 9:23–24).

The feast of Wisdom commences with Proverbs 10:1.

FOR FURTHER STUDY

1. What is the relationship between the wisdom of Proverbs and Jesus? Point out several significant areas of correspondence in Proverbs 8–9.
2. How is God portrayed as feeding his people elsewhere in the Old Testament (see Ps. 23; Isa. 55:1–2; 25:6)?

TO THINK ABOUT AND DISCUSS

1. Contrast the charms of Lady Wisdom in Proverbs 8 with those of the seductress in Proverbs 7.
2. Contrast the banquets offered by Lady Wisdom and Madame Folly in Proverbs 9.
3. What fundamental choices are you facing in your life which parallel the choices set forth in Proverbs 9?
4. How could you use Proverbs to bring the gospel to others?

7 The theology of Proverbs

The ten extended appeals for the son to seek wisdom in chapters 1–9 are followed by twenty-one chapters containing the pithy sayings that we commonly identify as 'proverbs'.

The sayings of chapters 10–30 jump from subject to subject and are often repetitive. While it would be possible to study their arrangement and to expound them consecutively, I believe it will be more effective to address this large section topically. In the following chapters, we will see how Proverbs addresses several crucial subjects.

The biblical Proverbs are unique

While other ancient and modern cultures have had their sayings of wisdom, the biblical book of Proverbs is unique because it goes beyond the pragmatic approach of other collections by declaring that true wisdom is rooted in the knowledge of God (1:7; 9:10). There is no wisdom without godliness. The ultimate problem of a fool is rooted in his or her attitude towards God. 'The foolishness of man ruins his way, and his heart rages against the LORD' (19:3).

The attributes of God are revealed in Proverbs

The study of Proverbs teaches us much about God's character. This is good because the greatest need of every human being is to know God. Many people view religion as a means by which they may achieve their goals as well as learn to better know and love themselves. The goal of Scripture, however, is that we would pursue God's goals as we learn to better know and love him. Many religious people today are idolaters. Even those who don't worship images of stone and wood commit idolatry by elevating man and promoting false ideas about God.

How can you know God?

God is transcendent and incomprehensible to the natural man. There is nothing in creation that can be compared to him (Isa. 40:18), which is why idols are strictly forbidden. The best works of man's hands (and mind) will only misrepresent and demean God. God is knowable because he has chosen to reveal himself both in his creation (natural revelation, as in 8:22–31) and in his Word (30:5). In this chapter we will consider how God's power, knowledge, justice, and grace are revealed in Proverbs.

God's omnipotence (power)

God is the almighty Creator

God's might is demonstrated in his creation, as he made all things out of nothing: 'The LORD by wisdom founded the earth, by understanding He established the heavens' (3:19;

8:22–36). He has made rich and poor (22:2). 'The hearing ear and the seeing eye, the LORD has made both of them' (20:12). Because we are his creatures, we are accountable to him. 'He who oppresses the poor taunts his Maker' (14:31).

God controls all things through his providence

We do not live in a world of chance, but rather our sovereign and omnipotent God is working out his purpose in every event. He is able to carry out all of his plans: 'Our God is in the heavens; He does whatever He pleases' (Ps. 115:3; see also Eph. 1:11; Jer. 32:27; Isa. 46:8–11). This is in sharp contrast to human beings, who often make plans that fail or have to be changed. The purpose of God always prevails: 'Many plans are in a man's heart, but the counsel of the LORD will stand' (19:21). God alone has an absolutely free will which cannot be thwarted by any force outside himself. He is the potter and we are the clay. God is sovereign even over the free acts of the mightiest of men: 'The king's heart is like channels of water in the hand of the LORD; He turns it wherever He wishes' (21:1). God even rules over the wicked and uses them for his own glory: 'The LORD has made everything for its own purpose, even the wicked for the day of evil'(16:4). God's omnipotence is also demonstrated in his sovereignty over inanimate objects: 'The lot is cast into the lap, but its every decision is from the LORD' (16:33).

Humble yourself before God

The sovereign power of God is not merely an abstract principle for theologians to debate: the fact that we serve an almighty God has many practical implications. First, we should be thankful that a personal God who loves us, rather than blind impersonal fate, is in control. We should also be humble. The natural man wants to think he is autonomous and in control of his own life. He doesn't want anyone, especially God, to take away his freedom or tell him what to do. Such human pride is an assault upon God's sovereignty. 'Everyone who is proud in heart is an abomination to the LORD; assuredly he will not be unpunished' (16:5). It is very foolish to oppose him, as Pharaoh, Haman, Balak, Herod, and many others can testify. 'There is no wisdom and no understanding and no counsel against the LORD' (21:30). 'Pride goes before destruction, and a haughty spirit before stumbling' (16:18). The wise man does not trust himself: 'He who trusts in his own heart is a fool, but he who walks wisely will be delivered' (28:26); nor does he fear or trust men: 'The fear of man brings a snare, but he who trusts in the LORD will be exalted'(29:25). Your success in life (education, career, relationships, family, church, government) depends entirely upon God. 'The horse is prepared for the day of battle, but victory belongs to the LORD'(21:31; see also John 15:5). You cannot bring your will to pass through your own skill and strength: 'Do not boast about tomorrow, for you do not know what a day may bring forth' (27:1). The fact that God is sovereign does not, however, mean that we are not

Your success in life (education, career, relationships, family, church, government) depends entirely upon God.

responsible for planning and taking action (21:5). As the pioneering missionary William Carey said, 'Expect great things from God. Attempt great things for God.'[15] Submit yourself to his moral will (wisdom) and his sovereign will, and you will succeed: 'Commit your works to the LORD and your plans will be established' (16:3).

God's omniscience (knowledge)

God is wise

God's perfect wisdom is contrasted with our ignorance: 'Surely I am more stupid than any man, and I do not have the understanding of a man. Neither have I learned wisdom, nor do I have the knowledge of the Holy One' (30:2–3). God's Word reveals his wisdom: 'Every word of God is tested; He is a shield to those who take refuge in Him' (30:5). God's perfect Word cannot be improved upon by human addition or change: 'Do not add to His words or He will reprove you, and you will be proved a liar' (30:6). God's revealed Word is both infallible and sufficient to meet all of our needs. Those who study his Word enjoy his blessing: 'He who gives attention to the word will find good, and blessed is he who trusts in the LORD' (16:20).

God knows everything

God knows everything comprehensively. He knows when a sparrow falls, and he knows the number of the hairs on your head (Matt. 10:29–30). God never learns and is never surprised, because his knowledge is eternal and infinite (Rom. 11:33–36).

God knows you

Proverbs teaches that God's knowledge is personal. He sees and takes interest in everything you do: 'The eyes of the LORD are in every place, watching the evil and the good' (15:3). This verse also implies God's omnipresence. There is no place you can go to hide from him (Ps. 139:7–9). God's knowledge of us is not merely abstract, it is moral: he knows not only what you do outwardly, but he sees the motives of your heart: 'Sheol and Abaddon lie open before the LORD, how much more the hearts of men!' (15:11). He knows you better than you know yourself and can see sins of which you are unaware, or for which you make excuses: 'All the ways of a man are clean in his own sight, but the LORD weighs the motives' (16:2); 'Every man's way is right in his own eyes, but the LORD weighs the hearts' (21:2). There is also a positive aspect to God's omniscience: God also sees and approves of the good things you do, even if no one else notices (Heb. 6:10).

Be humble about what you think you know

Compared with some folks, you may know a lot, but compared with God, you know nothing. Your knowledge is never comprehensive. Nor do you know what is best for your own sake. You must trust God that his way is the best possible way (3:5–6). God's knowledge should also move you to purify your heart. You can fool other people and perhaps even yourself, but you can never fool God: 'The ways of a man are before the eyes of the LORD, and He watches all his paths' (5:21). Hypocrisy is futile: 'The sacrifice of the wicked is an abomination, how much more when he brings it with evil intent!' (21:27). Ask God to show you the truth about yourself so that he might make you wise (Ps. 139:23–24). Also, we can marvel and rejoice that, even though God knows us exactly as we are, he still loves us in Christ.

God's justice

God is just

God's justice is implicit in virtually every line of Proverbs. Wisdom pays and folly destroys because God is just, 'guarding the paths of justice, and [preserving] the way of His godly ones' (2:8). His justice is expressed in his dealings with men. Even though, in the short term, the world may seem to be unfair because the wicked prosper and the righteous suffer, in the end the LORD will enact justice for all: 'The wages of the righteous is life, the income of the wicked, punishment' (10:16). It is very comforting to know that God is actively involved in all the affairs of men and that he will make all things right.

God's justice is perfect

Criminals sometimes escape earthly justice when human courts lack sufficient evidence. Sometimes they commit perjury, and the court believes their lies. But because God is all-knowing, his judgement is perfectly accurate: 'If you say, "See, we did not know this," does He not consider it who weighs the hearts? And does He not know it who keeps your soul? And will He not render to man according to his work?' (24:12). Often, the guilty go free on earth because of legal technicalities or mistakes. Occasionally, the righteous are falsely convicted, sometimes being exonerated years later by DNA evidence. The LORD, however, never acquits the guilty or punishes the innocent. Sometimes human courts fail to carry out their sentences because criminals flee their jurisdiction. Some murderers wait on death row for decades without being executed. But because God is all-powerful, his judgements are always carried out: 'Assuredly, the evil man will not go unpunished' (11:21*a*). He also brings blessing to those who are wise and righteous: 'The descendants of the righteous will be delivered' (11:21*b*); 'The righteous will be rewarded with prosperity' (13:21*b*). The culmination of God's justice will come on the last day, when all men shall stand before him and receive their due.

Because God is righteous, we do not need to become embittered over injustice.

Live in light of God's justice

You will never ever gain by sinning against God. When you choose to sin you are guilty of an unbelieving assault upon God's justice. You have deceived yourself into thinking that he will not see or that he will not act. On the positive side, you will never ever lose by acting wisely and doing his will: 'The fear of the LORD leads to life, so that one may sleep satisfied, untouched by evil' (19:23). Obedience takes faith because sometimes it may seem that you would benefit, at least in the short term, from telling a lie or indulging in a forbidden pleasure. God's justice also brings us comfort.

Because God is righteous, we do not need to become embittered over injustice. Nor is it our job to get even with those who harm us. Instead we should leave room for God's just wrath: 'Do not say, "I will repay evil"; wait for the LORD, and He will save you' (20:22; see also Rom. 12:17–21). We can trust him to protect us: 'The name of the LORD is a strong tower; the righteous runs into it and is safe' (18:10).

God's grace

The consideration of God's power, knowledge, and justice as revealed in Proverbs should cause us to tremble. God is holy (9:10; 30:3), and we are not. None of us meets the standards of wisdom and righteousness set forth in Proverbs: 'Who can say, "I have cleansed my heart, I am pure from my sin"?' (20:9). We all deserve his judgement because of our sin and folly. Proverbs declares that there is hope for sinners. God, as Wisdom, repeatedly calls out to sinners so that they may turn and live (1:20–23). He offers forgiveness to those who repent: 'He who conceals his transgressions will not prosper, but he who confesses and forsakes them will find compassion' (28:13). Proverbs even speaks of atonement for sin: 'By lovingkindness and truth iniquity is atoned for' (16:6*a*). What is revealed in part in Proverbs has been revealed in full in the New Testament. Jesus Christ has made atonement for the sins of all who believe in him. His death on the cross has fully satisfied the claims of God's justice against us. He gives us his perfect righteousness so that we are welcome in God's holy presence (1 Peter 3:18; 2 Cor. 5:21; Phil. 3:8–9). Praise God that his justice and mercy have met at the cross of Christ!

FOR FURTHER STUDY

1. What do the following texts add to the teaching of Proverbs about the sovereignty of God: Psalm 115:3; Jeremiah 32:27; Isaiah 45:1–2; Daniel 4:31–35; Revelation 17:14?
2. What do the following passages add to the teaching of Proverbs about God's knowledge: Psalm 19:8–10; 139:8; Isaiah 40:27–28; Matthew 10:29–30; Romans 11:33–36?
3. How does knowledge of the absolute sovereignty of God affect our approach to evangelism (see John 6:44; Acts 13:48)?

TO THINK ABOUT AND DISCUSS

1. How is the book of Proverbs different from the wisdom literature of other religions and cultures?
2. How can God control the actions of men without violating their freedom and responsibility (21:1)?
3. Where can the gospel be found in Proverbs?
4. In which attribute of God discussed in this chapter do you find the greatest comfort? Why?
5. How can a proper understanding of God's justice help us to face that which is unfair in this world?

8 Wisdom at work

There is no aspect of life on which we spend more time than our vocation. Your work establishes your identity and reflects your character. Proverbs teaches extensively about how wisdom can help you to enjoy success in your vocation.

The theology of work

The teaching of Proverbs about vocation must be put into the context of what the rest of Scripture says about work. The Bible begins with God's work of creation (Gen. 1:1–2:3). Jesus declares that God continues to work: 'My Father is working until now, and I myself am working' (John 5:17). God has created us to reflect his image through our work and to enjoy dominion on the earth through our labour (Gen. 2:1–3,15). Adam's Fall corrupted human labour. Work has become unpleasant as mankind must deal with 'thorns and thistles' such as drudgery, risk, and pain (Gen. 3:17–19). The Fall has also corrupted humanity so that some resist work through laziness and others oppress labourers (James 5:1–6). In the

New Testament, we learn that Christ reverses the effects of the Fall, thereby restoring labour as meaningful and significant before God (Eph. 6:5–8; 4:28).

Don't be a sluggard

Diligence is necessary for holiness. Laziness is a potentially life-destroying defect. Wisdom goes to great pains to exhort us to learn from the object lesson of the sluggard. When I walk around my neighbourhood, I notice that some homes are well cared for, with well-tended gardens. Other homes are dilapidated, with peeling paint and weeds growing tall in the yard, which brings the following verses to mind: 'I passed by the field of the sluggard and by the vineyard of the man lacking sense, and behold, it was completely overgrown with thistles; its surface was covered with nettles, and its stone wall was broken down. When I saw, I reflected upon it; I looked, and received instruction' (24:30–32). Plutarch said, 'Wise men profit more by fools than fools by wise men. For wise men will avoid the faults of fools, but fools will not imitate the virtues of wise men.'[16]

Characteristics of a sluggard

The sluggard is lazy (6:6)

Proverbs 6:6–10 contrasts the sluggard with the busy ant. The sluggard doesn't find significance in vocation; he looks upon work as an evil that is to be avoided. Wisdom mocks him, saying that he is so lazy he is weary of bringing his food from the dish to his mouth (26:15). He won't even cook his food (12:27).

The sluggard delights in sleep and recreation (6:9–10)

He doesn't get out of bed on time for work, perhaps because he was indulging his appetite for recreation late into the night. He knows he should get up, but 'as the door turns on its hinges, so does the sluggard on his bed' (26:14). When he finally does get out of bed he does as little as possible.

The sluggard lacks initiative (6:7)

In contrast to the busy ant, the sluggard won't do any work unless he is forced. As soon as the boss isn't looking, he is messing around (Eph. 6:6). When his supervisor is out of town, he comes in late and leaves early. He does the minimum amount of work. The only initiative he shows is in inventing excuses to avoid work: 'The sluggard says "There is a lion outside; I will be killed in the streets!"' (22:13). From time to time, sluggards come to the door of our church seeking financial help. When I question them about their work habits, they typically become very defensive and offer an avalanche of excuses. Spurgeon remarked, 'He [the sluggard] takes great pains to escape from pains.'[17] If the sluggard worked as hard at a job as he works at avoiding work, he might be rich!

The sluggard procrastinates (6:8)

In contrast to the ant, which prepares its food in the summer and gathers its provision in the harvest, the sluggard does not plough after the autumn, so he begs during the harvest and has nothing (20:4). His motto is 'Never do today what can be put off until tomorrow.'

The sluggard is self-deceived (6:9–10)

He doesn't realize he is a fool and actually believes his own excuses: 'I only need a little more sleep,' he says as he hits the snooze alarm for the fifth time. He has his own brand of wisdom: he says, 'Too much work hinders your enjoyment of life'; or, 'I have chosen to live a more noble and contemplative life'; or even, 'I want to serve God through study and prayer.' You cannot reason with him: 'The sluggard is wiser in his own eyes than seven men who can give a discreet answer' (26:16).

The sluggard is looking for easy money

He wants to get rich without diligence. He thinks he can circumvent God's way of gaining wealth through skill and hard work. He is a sucker for every get-rich-quick scheme. 'He who tills his land will have plenty of food, but he who follows empty pursuits will have poverty in plenty' (28:19). He is a dreamer and a talker, not a worker. 'In all labor there is profit, but mere talk leads only to poverty' (14:23). When his schemes fail, he expects the government, his family, and his friends to bail him out.

The sluggard is a destructive force

'He who is slack in his work is brother to him who destroys' (18:9). He is a poor steward of the valuable resources God has given him (24:30–31; see also Eccles. 10:18). He harms the business of the one who hires him: 'Like vinegar to the teeth and smoke to the eyes, so is the lazy one to those who send him' (10:26). Laziness can even destroy the economy of a nation when those who are working and being taxed can no longer support those receiving welfare. The sluggard also destroys families: his wife is frustrated and disheartened; his children are corrupted by his bad example. There are few more important factors in choosing a spouse than his or her attitude towards work.

God has ordained severe consequences for sluggardliness

'The way of the lazy is as a hedge of thorns' (15:19). The sluggard will be fired from his job. He will be poor: 'Your poverty will come in like a vagabond and your need like an armed man' (6:11); 'poor is he who works with a negligent hand' (10:4*a*); 'do not love sleep or you will become poor' (20:13*a*). A sluggard may even starve: 'An idle man will suffer hunger' (19:15*b*). Under the Old Covenant, a man who would not work to fulfil his obligations could even be sold into slavery: 'The slack hand will be put to forced labour' (12:24*b*). Men who cannot succeed in an unstructured job (such as sales) may need to work in a vocation that imposes structure and discipline upon them.

Under the Old Covenant, a man who would not work to fulfil his obligations could even be sold into slavery.

The sluggard will suffer many regrets. As he looks back upon his life, he will see unfulfilled ambitions, wasted opportunities, and failure (21:25–26*a*). He will experience unsatisfied desires, longing for what money can buy but having to live without: 'The soul of the sluggard craves and gets nothing' (13:4*a*). He will be disgraced in his family and in the community (10:5).

Don't provide material aid to sluggards

God disciplines sluggards by allowing them to experience the consequences of their folly with the desire that they will learn wisdom through their poverty: 'A worker's appetite works for him, for his hunger urges him on' (16:26). You subvert God's purpose and ultimately hurt the sluggard by enabling his sin. The same issue is raised in the New Testament when Paul says, 'If anyone is not willing to work, then he is not to eat, either' (2 Thes. 3:10*b*). Sluggards who live off the labour of others are thieves (20:4; Eph. 4:28). Old Covenant charity was given to the deserving poor who generally had to work for what they received, as in the case of Ruth, who gleaned (Ruth 2). Parents who give their young adult children food and shelter without requiring them to work are confirming them in their sluggardliness.

Be diligent

A man's character is demonstrated by how he approaches his vocation.

Characteristics of the wise worker

He works hard (6:6)

To the great distress of my dear wife, we occasionally experience an 'ant invasion' in our kitchen. While this is a practical inconvenience, it does give us an opportunity to 'observe her ways and be wise' (6:6*b*). If an ant finds even a morsel of food, suddenly the whole colony springs into action. Like a small army they march, cutting up the food and carrying off their prize. You will never see an ant standing still (unless you have sprayed it with insecticide). In the same way, those who are wise work wholeheartedly at all they do: 'Whatever your hand finds to do, do it with all your might' (Eccles. 9:10; see also Eph. 6:6*b*).

He takes initiative and works well without supervision (6:7)

Ants don't need a foreman to make sure they don't sleep on the job. Employers value employees who solve problems on their own and don't require constant oversight. Because the wise work to please God and not merely men, they work equally hard whether the eye of the boss is upon them or not (Eph. 6:6).

He prepares for the future (6:8)

Just as the ant prepares for the winter, so the wise worker is forward-thinking: 'The plans of the diligent lead surely to advantage' (21:5*a*). When he is young, he chooses a career that will utilize his abilities and by which he can provide well for his family. He then pursues the necessary training to be successful. He is willing to prove himself doing menial labour in the short term so that he can be promoted later.

He patiently pursues success

Unlike the sluggard who tries to get rich quickly, the wise worker is not distracted by get-rich-quick schemes (28:19). His formula for success is to gain valuable skills and to work hard. He plans to gradually build financial stability and wealth.

He is a good steward of his resources

In an agrarian economy, a wise worker would take care of his animals and fields: 'Know well the condition of your flocks, and pay attention to your herds, for riches are not forever' (27:23–24). A contemporary application would be that he keeps his work in good order and takes good care of his equipment. The office of a sluggard resembles the field of the lazy farmer (24:30–32).

He performs his duties with excellence and even artistry

'Do you see a man skilled in his work? He will stand before kings' (22:29). The Reformers rediscovered the biblical concept of vocation. You do not have to be a preacher or a missionary to serve God in your work, nor do you have to be a corporate CEO, a physician, or a high-powered lawyer to achieve significance. 'The milkmaid and the manure-hauler have the noblest of vocations,' said Luther, 'for they are doing God's work in the world.'[18] We are all full-time Christian workers, no matter what our vocation. The first biblical uses of the Hebrew word translated 'wisdom' speak of the persons skilled in creating garments for the high priest and building the tabernacle and the ark of the covenant (Exod. 28:3; 31:3,6; 35:26; 36:1–2). The wise man sees his vocation as being significant because he is imaging God's work of creation (Prov. 8:22–31). When engineers, electricians, or homemakers work wholeheartedly using their God-given skills, their work is highly honourable and worthy of recognition (Eph. 6:6; Col. 3:17,22–24).

God rewards the diligent

He will enjoy financial success

'The hand of the diligent makes rich' (10:4*b*). Some might argue that not all diligent people have lots of money. Remember, however, that the Proverbs are maxims which describe how the world works generally. Occasionally, sluggards win the lottery. Some diligent people face drought, disability, and other hard providences. Yet the maxim still applies: those who work hard usually prosper.

He will enjoy success and fulfilment in his vocation

'The hand of the diligent will rule' (12:24). His services will be in high demand. He will be promoted to positions of authority and responsibility. He will be respected in the community (22:29).

He will enjoy the fruit of his labour

Just as God took pleasure in his work of creation, so the wise worker will take pleasure in his daily accomplishments. As the result of his diligence, the labourer's appetite for food is satisfied (16:26) and his bills are paid. After having worked hard, he goes to bed content and with a clear conscience. 'The sleep of the working man is pleasant' (Eccles. 5:12).

He will be rewarded in the final judgement

Wise (skilled) workers don't just stand before kings; they will also stand before the King of kings. God won't honour just apostles, preachers, and missionaries on the Day of

Judgement: he will reward all those who honour him by their work (Eph. 6:8).

Proverbs does not promote communism

While the idealism of economic equality enjoyed by all through uniting to work for the common good may sound attractive, it does not work in the real world. Because of human depravity, some will not work hard unless they are forced. God has not ordained forced economic equality. Instead, his design is that the diligent prosper and the lazy suffer poverty. For governments to take money from the diligent so that they might provide for the lazy subverts God's design and is a form of theft.

Warnings to the diligent

Work is only good when it is exercised under God's lordship

'Commit your works to the LORD and your plans will be established' (16:3). Those who are skilled and successful are often tempted to feel proud, taking credit for what they have accomplished and boasting about what they will achieve in the future. Yet our success is totally dependent upon God's blessing. He will humble the proud.

Don't make work an idol

While Proverbs warns against laziness, some people go to the other extreme and put their careers ahead of the LORD. They are so intent on success that they neglect their families and God's gift of worship and rest on the Lord's Day. Your career is no substitute for your relationship with God, which should come first. 'The fear of the LORD is the beginning of wisdom' (9:10*a*). Ecclesiastes reminds us that the accumulation of wealth is vanity. You may be the fastest rat in the rat race, but when you die you will leave behind everything for which you laboured.

Exhortations to various classes of people

Young people should establish habits of diligence from an early age

> The work of a child is to prepare for adulthood through application to his or her education, helping at home

Work does not begin merely when you reach adulthood. The work of a child is to prepare for adulthood through application to his or her education, helping at home (10:5), and developing habits of self-discipline that will serve for life. Lazy children often become sluggard adults.

Homemakers should remain faithful in their work

The full-time wife and mother has one of the most challenging yet potentially rewarding of all vocations. The work of a homemaker is very challenging because her job is self-structured (and unpaid!). If she is not self-disciplined, her home will become a shambles (24:30–32). A lazy or disorganized woman places extra burdens on her husband and sets a terrible example for her children. On the other hand, when the homemaker excels, like the woman of Proverbs 31, she receives the praise of her husband, her children, and God.

Older people should continue working

Work should not end with retirement from your lifelong vocation. The person who no longer needs money should not devote his or her life to mere leisure (e.g. golf) but rather should continue to be productive for the Lord. There are tremendous opportunities for volunteering at church and in the community. The latter years of life can be among the most fruitful and fulfilling for the wise person.

Don't be a spiritual sluggard

Some of the fastest rats in the rat race for earthly success are lazy when it comes to the things of God. They neglect their souls the way the sluggard neglects his field. They have time to obtain top academic degrees but not to study God's Word. They have diligence to succeed in their business but lack the discipline to establish consistency in prayer and ministry. Like the sluggard, they make excuses: 'One day I will read the Bible seriously and get involved in the church.' On the last day, such wicked, lazy servants will be rebuked by the Lord for their failed spiritual stewardship (Matt. 25:26).

Conclusion

God has given you work to do for his glory

We are all workers in the Lord's vineyard. A wise person works not just for money but also to glorify God by exercising dominion in his image. We find fulfilment in pursuing our vocations with wisdom and excellence.

God gives you rest

While work is important, work is not to consume all of our time. God has blessed humanity with a weekly day of rest (Gen. 2:1–3; Exod. 20:8–11). He has made our work productive enough for us not to need to have to work every day to survive. Our weekly rest also reminds us of the spiritual rest we enjoy because of the finished work of Jesus Christ (Heb. 4:4–11). When it comes to salvation, we have rested from our own works and trust fully in his finished work for us. We look forward to everlasting rest in his presence.

FOR FURTHER STUDY

1. Compare the teaching about work in Proverbs to that contained in the New Testament (Eph. 6:5–9; Col. 3:22–4:1; Titus 2:9–10; 1 Peter 3:18–20).
2. How is God's pattern of work and rest in Genesis 1–2 a pattern for mankind?
3. How has the Fall affected human labour (Gen. 3:17–19)?

TO THINK ABOUT AND DISCUSS

1. Is every vocation equally honourable? Are there some vocations a wise person should avoid?
2. How do you plan to apply the principles in Proverbs so that you can enjoy greater success in your vocation?
3. What counsel would you give to someone who is unemployed or underemployed?
4. How can the government and the church help needy people without violating biblical principles?
5. How does the work of Christ bring us rest (see Heb. 4:4–11; Matt. 11:28–30)?
6. How can a believer find greater satisfaction in his or her work?

9 Financial wisdom

While Israel's greatest temptation was to worship the false idols of the nations, the god of this age is mammon. In the West, we live in a time of unprecedented prosperity. Sadly, many Christians worship the golden calf of materialism. Some churches and so-called ministries seem to be all about money—either raising money or promising their followers material prosperity.

Financial wisdom is one of the most heavily emphasized themes in Proverbs. Money is also the subject of many of Jesus' parables. There is no aspect of life which tests a man's character more than his attitude towards money (Luke 16:11). Proverbs trains us to have a correct attitude towards wealth and teaches us how to be wise as we acquire, spend, and save money. Most financial problems are spiritual problems.

The theology of money

God is the owner and source of all wealth. He owns 'the cattle on a thousand hills' (Ps. 50:10). 'It is He who is giving you power to make wealth' (Deut. 8:18). We are like tenant farmers on God's land. Proverbs teaches that God blesses the wise with prosperity: 'It is the blessing of the LORD that makes rich, and He adds no sorrow to it' (10:22). Abraham, Job, David, and Solomon all enjoyed great material blessing from God.

Are the wise always wealthy?

As we have already learned, the Proverbs are maxims which describe the way things generally turn out. Those who act wisely by earning money through hard work, by avoiding debt, and by carefully saving will generally prosper. Those who are lazy and overextend themselves with credit will generally suffer poverty. There will, however, be exceptions to the rule. Some fools are rich through gambling or an inheritance. Some wise people struggle to make ends meet. Another point is that the Proverbs were written during the days of the Old Covenant, under which material blessings were promised to Israel if the conditions of the covenant were kept (Deut. 28). There is no longer an earthly nation in covenant with God that can expect the material blessings of the covenant. Because we live as strangers in a hostile world, we may suffer economic persecution because of our faithfulness to God.

Because we live as strangers in a hostile world, we may suffer economic persecution because of our faithfulness to God.

A balanced view of money

An outstanding summary of financial wisdom is contained in 30:8–9, where the wise man prays that he will neither be so poor that he will be tempted to steal nor so rich that 'I ... deny You and say, "Who is the LORD?"'

Money can be good

Money itself is not evil. Paul tells us that it is the '*love* of money' that is 'a root of all sorts of evil' (1 Tim. 6:10). Proverbs teaches that it is beneficial to have wealth (8:21). The rich have more friends (14:20; 19:6). Solomon is not saying that this is right or that such friends are always worth having; rather, he is simply describing the realities of the world. Also, wealth can help you survive calamity (10:15). The rich can hire the best medical and legal help. They can more quickly recover from natural disasters. Also, money helps you fulfil your responsibilities to provide for your family (1 Tim. 5:8) and help those in need (Prov. 19:17). Furthermore, those with some money can enjoy more of the good things God has put into the world for us to enjoy with thankfulness (1 Tim. 4:3–4; 6:17). It is hard to be poor. Your friends and family may avoid you, perhaps because they fear you will want something from them (19:7). Those in poverty may be tempted to envy the rich or to steal (30:9*b*).

Money is dangerous

It is folly to make wealth your life's goal. In spite of what advertisers say, material things cannot satisfy your deepest spiritual appetites. Money can put food on the table, but it cannot put love around the table. 'Better is a dish of vegetables where love is than a fattened ox served with hatred' (15:17). Many are tempted to think, 'If I just had more money, or a new car, or a better house, I would be happy.' Some use money like a drug, buying themselves new possessions in the quest for happiness, but they are never satisfied (27:20; see also Isa. 55:1–2). The love of money leads to all kinds of other sins (1 Tim. 6:9–10). Each of the Ten Commandments has been broken because of money love. Another limitation of wealth is that it is fleeting: 'Do not weary yourself to gain wealth, cease from your consideration of it. When you set your eyes on it, it is gone. For wealth certainly makes itself wings like an eagle that flies toward the heavens' (23:4–5; see also 27:24). There are many stories of those who have squandered great fortunes (20:21). Even if you die rich, you will leave it all behind. It has been said that 'you never see an armoured car following a hearse'. The greatest threat posed by wealth is that the rich man can be tempted to become arrogant, trusting his money rather than God: 'He who trusts in his riches will fall' (11:28*a*; 1 Tim. 6:17). In Jesus' parable of the soils, the seed of the gospel is choked out by the deceitfulness of wealth (Matt. 13:22).

Godly wisdom is more important than wealth

It is better to seek wisdom in the fear of God than to be rich: 'Better is a little with the fear of the LORD than great treasure and turmoil with it' (15:16; see also 16:8; 17:1). Wisdom is to be valued above wealth: 'How much better it is to get wisdom than gold! And to get understanding is to be chosen above silver' (16:16). Waltke states, 'It [money] can buy a house, but not a home; it can put food on a table, but not fellowship around it.'[19] Your character is more important than your bank balance: 'A good name is to be more desired than great wealth, favor is better than silver and gold' (22:1). The fear of God brings peace and satisfaction (19:23). Wealth will be worthless on the Day of Judgement (11:4).

Learn the secret of contentment

We may expect God to provide for our needs: 'The LORD will not allow the righteous to hunger' (10:3*a*), but not necessarily all our desires. 'If we have food and covering, with these we shall be content' (1 Tim. 6:8). Because we know that God sovereignly distributes wealth according to his perfect will, we should be thankful and content with whatever he gives us (Prov. 10:22). 'Make sure that your character is free from the love of money, being content with what you have; for He Himself has said, "I will never desert you, nor will I ever forsake you"' (Heb. 13:5). One of the Puritans wrote, 'Contentment works not by adding to our circumstances, but by subtracting from our desires.'[20] The key to contentment is uniting our desires with God's will.

Acquiring money

Work hard

As we saw in the previous chapter, God's way for us to gain wealth is through obtaining a skill and working hard (10:4–5; 6:6–11). Don't expect others to provide for you (20:4). Don't expect easy money or fall prey to get-rich-quick schemes: 'He who tills his land will have plenty of food, but he who follows empty pursuits will have poverty in plenty' (28:19). Those who seek easy money are often impoverished in the process. Some people are very picky about the jobs they will accept, but not everyone is able to pursue his 'dream career'. There are certain jobs that attract far more seekers than there are opportunities. Some men drag their families through much misery and poverty because they won't face this reality. The wise man, however, has to be willing to do whatever is necessary to provide for himself and his family. Proverbs also teaches that man should first establish his means of earning before taking on major financial responsibilities (24:27).

Don't compromise your integrity to gain wealth

The person who has a strong desire to be rich will be tempted to sin: 'He who makes haste to be rich will not go unpunished' (28:20*b*); 'A man with an evil eye hastens after wealth and does not know that want will come upon him' (28:22). Some pursue wealth at the expense of family, worship, and rest. Many try to get rich by deceiving and defrauding others. They forget that a just God is watching over their business transactions. In ancient times, merchants would have two sets of weights, light and heavy, to use according to whether they were buying or selling, but 'differing weights and differing measures, both of them are abominable to the LORD' (20:10). God will judge those who deceive others by selling faulty products or using false advertising. 'The acquisition of treasures by a lying tongue is a fleeting vapor, the pursuit of death' (21:6).

While Proverbs does not promote socialism, wisdom sets standards that go beyond pure 'survival of the fittest' capitalism. It is wrong to use economic power to exploit the weak: 'He who oppresses the poor to make more for himself or who gives to the rich, will only come to poverty' (22:16). The wise man pays a fair wage to his workers and a reasonable price to his neighbour. The wise employee gives a full day's labour for a day's pay. Sometimes there are reports of a person obtaining a valuable antique for mere pennies at a jumble or rummage sale. Yet the wise man doesn't take advantage of the ignorance of others. '"Bad, bad," says the buyer, but when he goes his way, then he boasts' (20:14). Nor does he hoard a commodity in order to drive the price up so that he can extort more money from desperate buyers: 'He who withholds grain, the people will curse him, but blessing will be on the head of him who sells it' (11:26). Nor does he take advantage of the poor through usury: 'He who increases his wealth by interest and usury gathers it for him who is gracious to the poor' (28:8). He maintains his integrity because he believes that God will ultimately bring about justice: 'Bread obtained by falsehood is sweet to a man, but afterward his mouth will be filled with gravel' (20:17; see also Jer. 17:11).

Should Christians gamble and play the lottery?

Over six hundred billion dollars are spent on gambling in the United States per year, which is more money than is spent on groceries. Virtually every state runs a lottery, often claiming to use the proceeds for some good cause, such as education. But gambling is unwise and harmful. Gambling undermines the work ethic by encouraging people to hope for wealth without working for it (28:19). Gambling promotes irrationality in that the odds against winning a large prize are astronomical (14:23). Gambling is motivated by a greedy lust for riches (28:22,20; 1 Tim. 6:10,6). Gambling exploits those who lose (22:16). Gambling has harmful effects on society in terms of increases in crime, substance abuse, debt, suicide, and the breakup of families. Gambling is poor stewardship of God's resources. Only two things can happen when you gamble, and both are bad: you may lose, which means you have foolishly wasted your money; or you may win, in which case you have defrauded others by taking their money without earning it. Furthermore, you may be tempted to trust your wealth rather than God (30:9). There are many accounts of those who have won the lottery and, through folly, wound up penniless and friendless. 'Wealth obtained by fraud dwindles, but the one who gathers by labor increases it' (13:11; see also 10:2). 'He who profits illicitly troubles his own house' (15:27*a*). A gambler may say that he or she can gamble in moderation for recreation, but in so doing, he or she is supporting a destructive system that exploits others and is potentially making him- or herself vulnerable to an addiction. 'Do not participate in the unfruitful deeds of darkness, but instead even expose them' (Eph. 5:11).

Spending money

Give generously

'The generous man will be prosperous, and he who waters

will himself be watered' (11:25). We have already discussed the importance of giving to the Lord's work as the first priority in your budget (3:9–10); Proverbs also exhorts the wise man to be generous towards the deserving poor. 'One who is gracious to a poor man lends to the LORD, and He will repay him for his good deed' (19:17; see also 28:27). Charity is viewed not as a government programme but as a personal responsibility. Helping the needy requires balance. While we are not to give to sluggards (20:4), we are to be gracious to those who are in poverty—even if much of the fault is their own—providing they are willing to turn from folly and pursue wisdom. We are also warned not to give to the rich, who don't need our charity (22:16). God blesses those who are generous and wise: 'He who is generous will be blessed' (22:9*a*). This does not necessarily mean that those who give liberally will have riches to spend on themselves. Paul implies that God blesses those who are generous so that they can continue to be generous (2 Cor. 9:10–11).

The wise person shops with a list, not making impulsive or extravagant purchases.

Control your expenditures

The wise man lives by a budget, which is simply a plan for how he is going to allocate his money. 'The plans of the diligent lead surely to advantage' (21:5*a*). The fool runs out of money at the end of the month because he or she spent foolishly. 'Everyone who is hasty comes surely to poverty'

(21:5*b*). The wise person shops with a list, not making impulsive or extravagant purchases but only spending what his or her budget allows. Such a person develops sales resistance: 'The naive believes everything, but the sensible man considers his steps' (14:15). This person can't be taken in by salesmen who try to use flattery, feigned friendship, and pressure tactics (22:3). The wise person doesn't live beyond his or her means: 'He who loves pleasure will become a poor man, he who loves wine and oil will not become rich' (21:17). The wise person realizes that material things will not make him or her happy (Eccles. 2) and doesn't feel compelled to keep up with the neighbours. A wise man refuses to 'spend money he doesn't have to buy things he doesn't need to impress people he doesn't even like'.

Stay out of debt

Under the Old Covenant, debt was regarded as a curse (Deut. 28:44). Debt produces bondage to men: 'The borrower becomes the lender's slave' (22:7). Some are so burdened with debt that they spend many of their working hours earning money to pay their creditors. Those who buy on credit often pay high rates of interest which significantly increase the cost of their purchases. Debt also presumes upon the future: how can you know you will have more money in the future? 'The mind of man plans his way, but the LORD directs his steps' (16:9; see also James 4:13–17). The wise man pays his obligations promptly (3:27–28). What he spends is not determined by what he desires or the amount of credit he is offered but by his financial means. This is completely opposed to our consumer-driven economy, which is built on credit. Those who cannot resist overspending may be well advised to cut up their credit cards (Matt. 5:29).

Is it ever legitimate to borrow money?

Most people can't make major purchases, such as a house, with cash. Wisdom teaches us to establish ourselves financially before taking on major financial obligations such as a mortgage (24:27). The wise man takes pains to avoid putting himself into a situation in which he might not be able to pay his debts. When he does borrow, he doesn't put himself into a position in which he might owe more on an item than the amount for which he could sell it in an emergency. Because vehicles depreciate and real estate prices fluctuate, he makes large down payments so that he always has equity in what he owns. He may choose to grow his business more slowly rather than be highly leveraged with risky debt. The man of character repays all of his debts, not hiding behind a corporation or bankruptcy laws. 'The wicked borrows and does not pay back' (Ps. 37:21*a*).

Don't make yourself liable for the debt of others by co-signing

You may receive requests from family members or friends who want to finance a business, a home, an education, or a vehicle but cannot get a loan without a co-signer. In seeking your help, they may appeal to your love, your friendship, or even your vanity. The Proverbs contain repeated vivid pleas for us not to be surety for the debts of others: 'Do not be among those who give pledges, among those who become guarantors for debts. If you have nothing with which to pay, why should he take your bed from under you?' (22:26–27; see also 6:1–5). These warnings are not about helping a poverty-stricken brother. Instead we are warned against putting up our limited resources as collateral for the speculative ventures of others. If the banks won't lend them the money, they probably can't afford to take on the debt. You would be putting your credit and your family at risk. You may find yourself enslaved to the creditor. If you find yourself in this situation, do whatever you legitimately can to get out of it (6:3–5).

> **We are warned against putting up our limited resources as collateral for the speculative ventures of others.**

Saving money

Anticipate future expenses

One great way to avoid debt is to anticipate future expenses. During the time of harvest, the ant prepares for winter (6:8). Fools spend all of their income (and more) on payday. Those who are wise prepare for their children's education and for the winter of their retirement. They save for major future purchases so that they will not have to borrow and pay interest. Their savings provide protection from financial calamities such as unemployment, disability, or major car and home repairs (10:15). Seasons of prosperity (like Joseph's fat cow years in Genesis 41) should be times of preparation for possible lean years to come. A contemporary means of preparing for future calamity is to have adequate health, life, car, and home insurance.

Accumulate wealth and invest wisely

The wise person gradually and steadily accumulates savings through hard work and discipline (13:11). Such a person pays careful attention to his or her capital resources and investments (27:23–24). He or she is not suckered by scams promising sudden riches. A wise rule for investing is to remember that risk increases with anticipated rewards (28:19–20). If it sounds too good to be true, it is.

Is it wrong to receive interest from others?

It is absolutely forbidden to take advantage of the desperate need of another believer by charging high interest (28:8; see also Deut. 23:19). There is nothing wrong, however, with receiving interest from a legitimate investment (Deut. 23:20; Matt. 25:27).

Save so you can leave an inheritance to your children

A man who handles his finances with wisdom and integrity 'leaves an inheritance to his children's children' (13:22; see also 19:14; 2 Cor. 12:14). His children will be greatly helped along in life because of his financial acumen. He must also be careful to train them to handle money wisely or else 'an inheritance gained hurriedly at the beginning will not be blessed in the end' (20:21).

Conclusion

Make it your goal to be wise, not rich!

'Take my instruction and not silver, and knowledge rather

than choicest gold. For wisdom is better than jewels; and all desirable things cannot compare with her' (8:10–11). Material things will never satisfy you. 'He who loves money will not be satisfied with money, nor he who loves abundance with its income. This too is vanity' (Eccles. 5:10). Someone once asked a rich man, 'How much money is enough?' His reply was, 'Just a little more.' He was also quoted saying, 'I have made many millions, but they have brought me no happiness.' On the other hand, if you seek wisdom, your financial needs will also be met (10:3; Matt. 6:11).

You can't take it with you

My family lives within an hour's drive of Disneyland, where they sell 'Disney Dollars' with which purchases can be made inside the park. But when you leave Disneyland, you can't use Disney Dollars to buy petrol or a meal on your way home. When Christ returns, this present world will end and everything we have accumulated will be like Disney Dollars (2 Peter 3:10–13). On the other hand, the riches of the wise will endure forever because their treasure is in heaven (Matt. 6:19–21).

Remember Christ, who paid your debt

While God warns us against taking on the debts of others (6:1–5), he himself sent his Son to be surety for our sin. We owed an infinite debt because of our guilt. He took on our debt and paid it fully on the cross. Not only that, but he has also transferred his spiritual wealth to our account so that we are not merely debt-free, we are rich! 'For you know the grace of our Lord Jesus Christ, that though He was rich, yet for your sake He became poor, so that you through His poverty might become rich' (2 Cor. 8:9). Are you debt-free? Do you possess the riches of Christ?

FOR FURTHER STUDY

1. How have each of the Ten Commandments been broken by those who love money? (See 1 Tim. 6:10; Exod. 20:1–17.)
2. In what ways is money beneficial (see 1 Tim. 4:4–5)?

TO THINK ABOUT AND DISCUSS

1. Most of us have at some point prayed about our financial needs and desires. Have you ever prayed asking God not to make you too rich? Why pray this way (see 30:8–9)?
2. Why is debt bad (see 22:7)? Is it ever wise to borrow?
3. How much wealth is too much (see 10:22)? How do you decide what to give away?
4. What should it take for us to be content (see 1 Tim. 6:6–8)?
5. How rich do you have to be in order to give generously to the poor?
6. What is the definition of 'the deserving poor'?

10 Wise words

'Where there are many words, transgression is unavoidable, but he who restrains his lips is wise' (10:19). Researchers claim that the average person speaks over 15,000 words per day. The book of Proverbs recognizes the importance of our words by addressing this subject approximately 150 times in 915 verses (one-sixth of the book).

Words are powerful

There is a legend of a king who asked his trusted servant to bring him the most valuable object in his kingdom. The servant returned carrying, on a silver platter, a human tongue. The king then asked his servant to bring him the most dangerous object in the realm. The servant returned again with a human tongue. By words people and kingdoms can be built up or torn down: 'Death and life are in the power of the tongue' (18:21). 'By the blessing of the upright a city is exalted, but by the mouth of the wicked it is torn down' (11:11). James also speaks of the tongue as a powerful force for good or for evil (James 3:1–12).

God reveals himself to us using language (2 Tim. 3:16–17), and it is through preaching that God's Word is spread and lives are transformed (2 Tim. 4:1–6). On the other hand, through words error is spread and lives are ruined.

Words are limited

Words are no substitute for action. Some people are great talkers but poor doers. 'In all labor there is profit, but mere talk leads only to poverty' (14:23; see also James 1:22). Words alone cannot change a heart. You cannot reason with some people: 'A slave will not be instructed by words alone; for though he understands, there will be no response' (29:19). Action may sometimes be needed to ensure the desired response from those who are unwise: 'On the lips of the discerning, wisdom is found, but a rod is for the back of him who lacks understanding' (10:13).

Words reveal what is in your heart

Speech is among the truest indicators of whether a person's character is wise or foolish. Just as you discover what is in a jar by pouring out its contents, so when a person opens his or her mouth, the contents of his or her heart pour out. 'The tongue of the wise makes knowledge acceptable, but the mouth of fools spouts folly' (15:2). 'The mouth of the righteous flows with wisdom, but the perverted tongue will be cut out' (10:31). Jesus said, 'The mouth speaks out of that which fills the heart' (Matt. 12:34). If our hearts are right, our speech will be wise. 'Watch over your heart with all diligence, for from it flow the springs of life' (4:23). We speak in the image of God, who speaks in creation and in his Word.

Every time we open our mouths we are either advancing God's agenda or that of the evil one.

Don't use your speech to destroy

'With his mouth the godless man destroys his neighbor' (11:9). 'The words of the wicked lie in wait for blood' (12:6*a*). 'A worthless man digs up evil, while his words are like scorching fire' (16:27).

Flattery

'A man who flatters his neighbor is spreading a net for his steps' (29:5). Flattery is telling people what they want to hear, but for selfish ends. You can be ruined if you listen to flattery (26:28*b*). The smooth-talking salesman flatters his customer so that he can get a commission. The adulteress seduces her victims through flattery (2:16). The powerful businessman or politician is surrounded by 'yes men' who are more concerned about advancing their own careers than giving wise advice. Flattery which is not malicious can be harmful. For example, church members who offer insincere praise for the mediocre sermon of a young layman may encourage him to devote his life to a ministry for which he lacks the necessary gifts and calling.

Flattery which is not malicious can be harmful.

Lies

'Lying lips are an abomination to the LORD' (12:22*a*). Liars selfishly manipulate words to help themselves and harm others. They lie because they want to avoid the consequences of their sinful acts or because they want to deceitfully get something from others. 'A lying tongue hates those it crushes' (26:28*a*; see also 6:19; 26:26). Those who commit perjury to protect themselves and their friends or to harm their enemies undermine justice: 'A rascally witness makes a mockery of justice' (19:28*a*). 'Like a club and a sword and a sharp arrow is a man who bears false witness against his neighbor' (25:18). Proverbs also warns against deceiving others with cruel jokes (26:18–19).

Gossip and slander

Because of our depravity, we tend to enjoy gossip. 'The words of a whisperer are like dainty morsels, and they go down into the innermost parts of the body' (18:8). We like to be 'in the know'. We are guilty of gossip when what we pass on to others is not fitting to repeat, even if it is true. 'He who goes about as a talebearer reveals secrets, but he who is trustworthy conceals a matter' (11:13; see also 17:9). Slander destroys people and relationships: 'A perverse man spreads strife, and a slanderer separates intimate friends' (16:28). Shakespeare wrote in Othello, 'He who steals my purses steals trash, but he that filches my good name … makes me poor indeed.'[21] Some use gossip to get revenge on an enemy. Gossip is like a contagious disease. The wise avoid those who gossip and refuse to spread the disease by repeating gossip (20:19; 26:20).

Angry speech

'Do not be eager in your heart to be angry, for anger resides in the bosom of fools' (Eccles. 7:9). Anger stems from pride and selfishness (James 4:1–2*a*). Angry people wrongfully play God, pouring out their vengeance on those who have offended them (but see Rom. 12:19). Their anger is not a righteous zeal for the glory of God but a passion to vindicate themselves. Their angry words and acts express the murder that resides in their hearts (Matt. 5:21–22). The angry person is out of control and vulnerable to many other transgressions: 'Like a city that is broken into and without walls is a man who has no control over his spirit' (25:28; see also Eph. 4:26–27). Anger impairs judgement: 'A quick-tempered man acts foolishly' (14:17*a*). Angry words wound deeply: 'There is one who speaks rashly like the thrusts of a sword' (12:18*a*). Hateful speech can escalate into violent acts: 'A hot-tempered man abounds in transgression' (29:22*b*). Those who are angry often stir up strife (15:18). The wise avoid people given to anger (22:24).

Quarrelsome speech

Closely related to angry speech are words which stir up strife: 'A fool's lips bring strife' (18:6*a*; see also 28:25; 13:10; 10:12). Some people seem to enjoy argumentation: 'He who loves transgression loves strife' (17:19*a*); 'like charcoal to hot embers and wood to fire, so is a contentious man to kindle strife' (26:21). Some homes are miserable because of constant bickering: 'Better is a dry morsel and quietness with it than a house full of feasting with strife' (17:1). Those who are wise avoid conflict and refuse to add fuel to the fire of strife: 'The beginning of strife is like letting out water, so abandon the quarrel before it breaks out' (17:14). There are several warnings against a quarrelsome woman who nags her husband: 'It is better to live in a desert land than with a contentious and vexing woman' (21:19; see also 19:13; 21:9; 25:24; 27:15–17). It is often wise to drop certain issues, even among friends and family, when an impasse is reached. It is unwise to argue with fools or to dispute with those whose mind is already made up (26:4).

Perverse speech

The wise don't use filthy or inappropriate speech: 'He who is perverted in his language falls into evil' (17:20*b*).

Proud speech

Because they humbly recognize God's sovereignty, the wise do not boast about what they will do or have done: 'Do not boast about tomorrow, for you do not know what a day may bring forth. Let another praise you, and not your own mouth; a stranger, and not your own lips' (27:1–2). This text might be appropriate to review before one writes a Christmas letter.

Excessive speech

'The one who guards his mouth preserves his life; the one who opens wide his lips comes to ruin' (13:3). We are far more likely to get into trouble for saying too much than for not speaking enough: 'When there are many words, transgression is unavoidable, but he who restrains his lips is wise' (10:19); 'even a fool, when he keeps silent, is considered wise; when he closes his lips, he is considered prudent' (17:28). The advent of e-mail also brings new risks. People sitting alone with their computers tend to be more careless with their words than they would be in the presence of others. We should hesitate and think before speaking or writing. 'Do you see a man who is hasty in his words? There is more hope for a fool than for him' (29:20; James 1:19).

God judges foolish speech

Because God is sovereign and just, those who misuse their tongues suffer the consequences both now and in the final judgement: 'The eyes of the LORD preserve knowledge, but He overthrows the words of the treacherous man' (22:12); 'the perverted tongue will be cut out' (10:31*b*); 'a babbling fool will be ruined' (10:10*b*); 'a fool's mouth is his ruin, and his lips are the snare of his soul' (18:7); 'his mouth calls for blows' (18:6*b*); 'an evil man is ensnared by the transgression of his lips' (12:13); 'in the mouth of the foolish is a rod for his back' (14:3*a*; see also 19:5,9,19). Jesus also taught that we will be judged for what we say: 'Every careless word that people speak, they shall give an accounting for it in the day of judgement. For by your words you will be justified, and by your words you will be condemned' (Matt. 12:36–37).

Learn to speak with wisdom

The tongue, which can destroy, can also build up when used wisely.

Exercise self-control

While the fool blurts out whatever he or she thinks or feels, the wise person controls his or her words: 'He who guards his mouth and his tongue, guards his soul from troubles'

(21:23). The wise person listens to others before he or she speaks: 'A fool does not delight in understanding, but only in revealing his own mind' (18:2); 'He who gives an answer before he hears, it is folly and shame to him' (18:13; see also James 1:19). The one who is wise doesn't jump to conclusions: 'The first to plead his case seems right, until another comes and examines him' (18:17). He doesn't have to have the last word (10:19). He is slow to anger and avoids disputes: 'A fool always loses his temper, but a wise man holds it back' (29:11); 'the slow to anger calms a dispute' (15:18*b*); 'he who is slow to anger has great understanding' (14:29*a*); 'like one who takes a dog by the ears is he who passes by and meddles with strife not belonging to him' (26:17). When wronged, the wise either overlook the sin (19:11*b*) or seek to restore those in the wrong by confronting them privately (Gal. 6:1; Matt. 18:15). Because they trust God to bring about justice, they refuse to seek revenge (20:22; Rom. 12:19). Because they have been freely forgiven by God in Christ, they are ready to forgive others (Eph. 4:32).

Speak with integrity

'Truthful lips will be established forever' (12:19*a*). The wise man is characterized by integrity. When called upon to give testimony, he tells the truth, the whole truth, and nothing but the truth: 'A truthful witness saves lives' (14:25*a*). When he makes a promise, he keeps his word, even if it costs him dearly: 'He swears to his own hurt and does not change' (Ps. 15:4*c*). Even when he might be able to fool men and thus benefit in the short run, he is honest because he knows that God hears every word he speaks.

Build others up with your words

Everything we say should edify others and honour God (Eph. 4:29). By words we teach wisdom to others: 'The lips of the wise spread knowledge' (Prov. 15:7*a*); 'the teaching of the wise is a fountain of life' (13:14*a*). Of the godly wife it is said: 'She opens her mouth in wisdom and the teaching of kindness is on her tongue' (31:26). Words can be used to give wise counsel: 'Oil and perfume make the heart glad, so a man's counsel is sweet to his friend' (27:9). By speech we can evangelize the lost: 'The fruit of righteousness is a tree of life, and he who is wise wins souls' (11:30; see also Matt. 28:18–20). By words of rebuke we can deliver others from sin: 'He who rebukes a man will afterward find more favor than he who flatters with the tongue' (Prov. 28:23). 'Faithful are the wounds of a friend, but deceitful are the kisses of an enemy' (27:6). We can offer encouragement to the downcast: 'Anxiety in a man's heart weighs it down, but a good word makes it glad' (12:25). By speech we can deliver the oppressed: 'Open your mouth for the dumb, for the rights of all the unfortunate. Open your mouth, judge righteously, and defend the rights of the afflicted and needy' (31:8–9). Sometimes it is sinful to remain silent: 'Better is open rebuke than love that is concealed' (27:5). The wise speak their love to their spouses, their children, and their friends.

By words of rebuke we can deliver others from sin.

Develop excellence in the manner of your speech

Wisdom is concerned not merely about what is said, but also about the way in which it is said. The world may say, 'Fight fire with fire.' Wisdom says, 'Usually it is best to fight fire with water.' 'A gentle answer turns away wrath, but a harsh word stirs up anger' (15:1); 'sweetness of speech increases persuasiveness' (16:21*b*). The timing of what we say can greatly enhance our message: 'Like apples of gold in settings of silver is a word spoken in right circumstances' (25:11). A wise wife may wait to bring the troubles of the day to her tired husband until after he has had time to enjoy his dinner and relax for a few minutes. But 'He who blesses his friend with a loud voice early in the morning, it will be reckoned as a curse to him' (27:14; see also 25:20). We are not only to be excellent speakers, but also wise listeners: 'A plan in the heart of a man is like deep water, but a man of understanding draws it out' (20:5). Those who speak well are persuasive: 'By forbearance a ruler may be persuaded, and a soft tongue breaks the bone' (25:15).

God values and rewards wise speech

'The tongue of the righteous is as choice silver' (10:20*a*). Wise words bless those who hear: 'Pleasant words are like a honeycomb, sweet to the soul and healing to the bones' (16:24); 'the lips of the righteous feed many' (10:21*a*); 'a soothing tongue is a tree of life' (15:4). By speaking well we do God's work of spreading wisdom. God blesses those who speak well: 'With the fruit of a man's mouth his stomach will be satisfied. He will be satisfied with the product of his lips'

(18:20). Wise speech pays off in relationships, in your vocation, and in eternity (12:14; 13:2).

Conclusion

How can you change your speech?

The reason our speech gets us into trouble has little to do with the tongue. We sin in our speech because we are sinners by nature who don't properly fear God. Before your speech patterns can be changed, your heart must be transformed (4:23; Matt. 12:34–35).

Christ speaks to you

One of the names of Jesus is 'the Word' (John 1:1; see also Prov. 8:6–7). He is the perfect and final revelation from God. When on earth, he was the master of wise speech. Never once did he flatter, lie, gossip, or speak with sinful anger. Even when people tried to entrap or provoke him, 'while being reviled, He did not revile in return … but kept entrusting Himself to Him who judges righteously' (1 Peter 2:23). Every word Jesus spoke was true. Out of his mouth flowed wisdom (10:31*a*; John 7:38). His wise words continue to build up and give life to those who listen (John 6:63). Just as in Proverbs a sagacious king teaches wisdom to his people, King Jesus teaches you how to become wise and speak well. Ask God for wisdom through Christ, and he will answer abundantly (James 1:5).

FOR FURTHER STUDY

1. What characteristics of wise speech can be observed in Jesus' words in the Sermon on the Mount (Matt. 5–7)?
2. Compare the teaching of James 3:1–6 to what Proverbs says about the tongue.

TO THINK ABOUT AND DISCUSS

1. Why isn't it true that 'sticks and stones can break my bones, but words will never hurt me'?
2. What is the difference between gossip and the legitimate exchange of information among concerned parties?
3. How can listening to people's speech help you to choose your friends?
4. When have your careless words gotten you into trouble?
5. Is there any such thing as a 'white lie'?
6. In what practical ways can you use your speech to build others up: in your family, at church, and in your workplace?

11 Wise child training

Our culture's children are in trouble. Newspapers report alarming rates of crime, substance abuse, gang membership, teen pregnancy, and illiteracy among minors. Politicians debate how these problems might be solved through public education and government programmes.

Among the many modern theories of education, one is overlooked. The book of Proverbs tells us exactly what the problem with our children is and how it can be addressed: children lack wisdom. As parents are primarily responsible for training their sons and daughters, children must heed the instruction of their parents.

Discipline your children

Why is discipline necessary?

'Foolishness is bound up in the heart of a child' (22:15*a*). Children need discipline because they are by nature foolish (morally deficient and lacking in sense). Scripture teaches that children are neither good nor innocent (like blank slates) from birth; rather, they are conceived with a sinful, wayward nature: 'The intent of man's heart is evil from his youth' (Gen. 8:21*b*; see also Ps. 51:5). Some worldly 'experts' say that children should be left free to express themselves as they wish, but Proverbs warns, 'A child who gets his own way brings shame to his mother' (29:15*b*). Because of Adam's Fall, if I were to let my garden go its own way I would have weeds, thorns, and thistles, not flowers and fruit. In the same way, if I leave my child undisciplined, nothing but folly will grow. Below is a list of some of the characteristics of foolishness as defined in Proverbs which parents must resist in their children.

- Fools reject wisdom and instruction (15:5; 1:7,22,32; 10:8; 18:2; 30:11,17; 20:20).
- Fools don't respect their parents (19:26; 30:17).
- Fools choose foolish and wicked companions (13:20; 14:7; 22:24).
- Fools talk too much (12:23; 13:16; 15:2; 18:7; 29:11,20).
- Fools are boastful (27:1–2).
- Fools are proud (14:16; 28:26).
- Fools justify their sin (12:15; 28:26).
- Fools are self-centred (18:2).
- Fools are quick-tempered (12:16,18; 14:17,29).
- Fools are argumentative and quarrelsome (18:6; 20:3; 26:4–5; 29:9).
- Fools gossip and tattle (11:13; 20:19).
- Fools get into mischief (10:23).
- Fools mock at sin (14:9).
- Fools are stubborn (17:10).

- Fools are unreliable (26:6).
- Fools flatter and manipulate (29:5).
- Fools are lazy (10:5).
- Fools lie (12:22; 26:18–29).
- Fools steal (28:24).
- Fools are unwise with money (14:24; 28:24).
- Fools are immoral (7:22; 29:3).
- Fools abuse intoxicating substances (23:29–35).
- Fools are gluttons (28:7).

Foolishness is deadly, like a cancerous tumour, and must be removed. Because folly is 'bound up' in the heart of a child, it will not come out easily. Thick chains won't be loosed by mere words, much less by weak methods such as parental whining or bribery.

God has given the rod of discipline as a tool to remove folly from a child's heart

'Foolishness is bound up in the heart of a child; the rod of discipline will remove it far from him' (22:15). God has given parents a tool, a key to loose the chains of foolishness, a surgeon's knife to cut the cancer out. This tool is the rod of discipline. Parents act as God's agents when they chastise their children. Our discipline of our children should emulate God's perfect discipline of us (3:11–12). Discipline should be carried out lovingly and tenderly (4:3–4; Ps. 103:13). The Word of God defines the foolishness (see the above list) that is to be addressed through discipline.

Discipline is a test of your love for your child and your trust in God

Some parents, under the influence of worldly psychology,

say, 'I love my children too much to spank them.' Scripture, however, says that disciplining a child is an act of love and that parents who refuse to resist the foolishness of their children actually hate them: 'He who withholds his rod hates his son, but he who loves him disciplines him diligently' (13:24). God disciplines us because he loves us: 'For whom the LORD loves He reproves, even as a father corrects the son in whom he delights' (3:12). Neglect of discipline is among the worst forms of child abuse. The question is whether you will trust God or whether you will lean on your own understanding (3:5–6). Just as the pain of the vaccination needle is worthwhile because it can save your child from a deadly disease, so discipline is painful in the short term, both for the child and the parent, but the result, wisdom (or 'the peaceful fruit of righteousness', Heb. 12:11), is worth it. When I was in college, I was very impressed by the way in which the pastor of our church was training his young son and daughter. One day I asked the children, 'Why do your parents spank you?' They both cheerfully replied, 'Our parents spank us because they love us.'

Neglect of discipline is among the worst forms of child abuse.

How to carry out biblical discipline

It is hard work to diligently and faithfully discipline your child (13:24). Discipline is often time-consuming and inconvenient. Your child may misbehave at the most inopportune moment. He or she may be testing you, trying to get away with folly when you are very busy or out in public. You cannot allow your child to manipulate his or her way out of deserved chastisement: 'Do not hold back discipline from the child, although you strike him with the rod, he will not die. You shall strike him with the rod and rescue his soul from Sheol' (23:13–14). Some parents get worn down after many years and many children. Or they may get discouraged by the apparent lack of results. But as long as the child is living at home, you can't give up: 'Discipline your son while there is hope, and do not desire his death' (19:18). It is also important that both parents be committed to the same standards and methods of discipline or your child will divide and conquer, playing mother and father off against each other (Matt. 12:25). Wayward children are wise in their own eyes (Prov. 3:7). Parents should not waste time quarrelling with such children (20:3) but should take corrective action. You do not need to get your child to agree with your standards or your discipline. As children get older, it may be appropriate to inflict pain through means other than the rod, such as hard work or severe restrictions on privileges.

Don't misuse discipline

'Fathers, do not exasperate your children, so that they will not lose heart' (Col. 3:21). Foolishness and rebellion, not childishness, should be chastised. If your toddler accidentally knocks his or her cup of milk off the table, this is childishness and shouldn't be punished. On the other hand, if he or she looks you in the eye and hurls the cup across the kitchen, it is foolishness and time to get the rod. Do not discipline in anger. An out-of-control parent sets a poor example by his or her foolish anger (16:32) and is at risk of physically abusing the child. Before you can control a child, you must first control yourself. The purpose of discipline is to train your child, not avenge yourself (Rom. 12:19).

Apply both the rod and reproof

'The rod and reproof give wisdom' (29:15*a*). Discipline must be accompanied by verbal admonition so that the child will know why he or she is being chastised. When a child listens to parental instruction, the rod is not necessary. 'A rebuke goes deeper into one who has understanding than a hundred blows into a fool' (17:10). Ideally, as a child gets older, the rod will be used increasingly rarely. On the other hand, sometimes verbal reproof will not be enough. A mother came to me once saying, 'My child won't listen to biblical counsel.' Proverbs explains what must be done in such cases: 'A rod is for the back of him who lacks understanding' (10:13); 'strokes reach the innermost parts' (20:30*b*). I am told that there was an ancient Near Eastern proverb that said, 'Boys have their ears on their backsides.' Eli is a sad example of parental failure, because he rebuked his sons but did not take action against their wickedness (1 Sam. 2:22–25).

Impart wisdom to your children by teaching them

If discipline is like pulling weeds from your garden, instruction is like planting flowers.

Education takes place in the home

The book of Proverbs presents a model of a godly home in

which the father faithfully instructs his children. The ten introductory discourses are addressed to a son (1:8; 2:1; 3:1; 4:1,10,20; 5:1; 6:1,20; 7:1), appealing for him to commit his life to seeking wisdom. The collections of proverbs that begin in chapter 10 form the content of the wisdom that parents are to teach to their children. Sadly, many parents are guilty of abdicating their role of teacher to the government or even the church. While parents may use outside teachers to supplement the teaching that takes place in the home, they are not to delegate this duty to others. Both mother and father are to be involved in teaching their sons and daughters (1:8).

The goal of parental instruction is to mould character

It is not enough to merely control your children's behaviour while they are in the home: your goal is to shape the inner character so that they will live wisely once grown up and living on their own. The father in Proverbs prepares the son for adulthood and independence by telling him how to restrain his tongue, manage his career, handle his money, avoid sexual immorality, and choose a wife. He seeks to encourage qualities of honesty, self-control, generosity, diligence, and respect for authority. There is no such thing as a 'secular' education; every practical issue is a moral issue that must be approached from the standpoint of the fear of the LORD (1:7). Parents hope to build wise convictions in their children so that they will make wise choices even when no one is looking or forcing them to comply. Godly character is not a list of dos and don'ts but skill to make wise decisions in every situation in life.

Formal and informal instruction

'These words, which I am commanding you today, shall be on your heart. You shall teach them diligently to your sons and shall talk of them when you sit in your house and when you walk by the way and when you lie down and when you rise up' (Deut. 6:6–7). In order for a father to successfully teach his children, God's Word must first be on his own heart. You cannot expect to successfully impart wisdom to your children unless you personally love wisdom and devote yourself to God's Word. Then you will have the discipline and desire to have regular Bible reading and study with your children. You will also use everyday situations outside the home (while driving around or shopping) to instruct your children. Your example of how you spend your time, manage your money, and control your tongue will also speak volumes to your children.

Children should honour their parents

Embrace discipline and instruction

The child who has parents who are devoted to raising him or her in the nurture and admonition of the Lord is uniquely blessed. Children, recognize and admit the folly bound up in your own heart and cooperate with your parents in the battle to build your character (22:15). Don't resist their discipline, but embrace it: 'A fool rejects his father's discipline, but he who regards reproof is sensible' (15:5; see also 3:11–12). Don't harden your heart or fight discipline through arguing: 'He who hates reproof will die' (15:10*b*). You are like a diamond in the rough, and your parents are God's tools for shaping and refining you. Honour your parents by listening carefully to their teaching: 'My son, observe the commandment of your father and do not forsake the teaching of your mother; bind them continually on your heart; tie them around your neck. When you walk about, they will guide you; when you sleep, they will watch over you … For the commandment is a lamp and the teaching is light; and reproofs for discipline are the way of life' (6:20–23). Ask for forgiveness when you sin (28:13). Express appreciation for their labours and sacrifices on your behalf (31:28). The worst thing that could happen to you would be for you to wear them out so that they give up and leave you to your own way.

Honour your parents in their old age

Adult offspring are no longer to be disciplined as children. Nor are they still required to render absolute obedience to parents. They still, however, owe their parents respect. One important way in which we honour our parents is to make sure their needs are met in their old age. Provision for the elderly begins with the family and should not be left to the state. Jesus rebuked the hypocrites who failed to fulfil the fifth commandment by providing for their aged parents (Matt. 15:3–6; see also Prov. 19:26). Paul says that the person who doesn't provide for his or her own needy relatives is 'worse than an unbeliever' (1 Tim. 5:8). Even if your parents have plenty of financial resources, you can still show them honour by ensuring that their non-material needs are being met through visiting, calling, writing, and praying for them.

Bring joy to your parents

The happiness of parents is bound up in their children: 'A wise son makes a father glad, but a foolish son is a grief to his mother' (10:1). Your righteousness will give your parents great joy. 'The father of the righteous will greatly rejoice, and he who sires a wise son will be glad in him. Let your father and your mother be glad, and let her rejoice who gave birth to you' (23:24–25). Your folly will make them miserable in their old age: 'He who sires a fool does so to his sorrow, and the father of a fool has no joy … A foolish son is a grief to his father and bitterness to her who bore him' (17:21,25). In the New Testament, John writes, 'I have no greater joy than this, to hear of my children walking in the truth' (3 John 1:4).

Honour your parents or else …

Our sovereign and just God will judge those who reject parental wisdom: 'He who curses his father or his mother, his lamp will go out in time of darkness' (20:20); 'the eye that mocks a father and scorns a mother, the ravens of the valley will pick it out and the young eagles will eat it' (30:17).

Why are some children wayward?

Does wise parenting guarantee wise kids?

Many look upon Proverbs 22:6—'Train up a child in the way he should go, even when he is old he will not depart from it'—as an absolute and unconditional promise. They believe that they can, by following the formula laid out in Scripture, ensure the conversion of their children. Sadly, they forget that the Proverbs are maxims that describe how things generally, but not always, turn out. As we saw when looking at 10:4, not all lazy people are poor and not all diligent people are rich. Similarly, when it comes to parenting, there is no absolute guarantee of success. Our children are foolish by nature and would forever reject wisdom apart from a work of God's sovereign grace (Gen. 8:21). We are imperfect parents (Heb. 12:10) who would ruin our children, even if they were blank slates. None of us is a good enough parent to merit our children's salvation.

Why do kids turn out the way they do?

There are three factors that determine how a child turns out. First, parents are responsible for disciplining and instructing their children faithfully. Parents who neglect their duty contribute to the ruin of their offspring (13:24). The second factor is that children are responsible for the choices they make: 'It is by his deeds that a lad distinguishes himself, if his conduct is pure and right' (20:11). Not all rebellion is the fault of parents. Cain and Abel grew up in the same environment with the same parents. Abel worshipped God, while Cain rejected direct admonition from God and murdered his brother (Gen. 4:1–6). The story of the first human family has been repeated many times. The entire book of Proverbs is a plea to a son to choose wisdom over folly. The parent can present the truth, but he or she can't make the child believe. The child who rejects wisdom bears the consequences of his or her folly. The LORD himself knows what it is like to have a wayward child: 'Listen, O heavens, and hear, O earth; for the LORD speaks, "Sons I have reared and brought up, but they have revolted against Me"' (Isa. 1:2). Israel, like Cain, rejected God's discipline: 'In vain I have struck your sons; they accepted no chastening ... You have smitten them, but they did not weaken; you have consumed them, but they refused to take correction. They have made their faces harder than rock; they have refused to repent' (Jer. 2:30*a*; 5:3). The third and ultimate factor in determining how children turn out is God's sovereign grace. Only he can soften a hard heart and give sight to the blind. If your children are walking with the Lord, give him glory. (For more information on the subject of dealing with wayward children, see *When Good Kids Make Bad Choices* by Elyse Fitzpatrick and Jim Newheiser, Harvest House, 2005.)

Conclusion: Train your children in wisdom

What do you want most for your children: beauty, education, status, and wealth? Or is your greatest desire that they be wise? Bridges writes, 'Most people deal with their children as if they were born only for the world ... They educate them for time, not for eternity.'[22] Devote yourself to training your children to fear God and to walk in his wisdom. The work is hard, but the potential reward is great.

FOR FURTHER STUDY

1. How does the teaching in Proverbs about child training compare with the expectations of parents and children taught in the law? (See Deut. 6:4–9; Exod. 20:12.)
2. Find parallels between the teaching in Proverbs and that in the New Testament on the responsibilities of children and parents. (See Eph. 6:1–4; Matt. 15:3–6.)

TO THINK ABOUT AND DISCUSS

1. How does the teaching of Proverbs about child training compare with the views propounded by mainstream psychologists?
2. To what extent may parents delegate their responsibility to train their children?
3. What is the difference between a biblical use of the rod to spank children and child abuse?
4. What should parents do if the government places a legal ban on spanking? (See Acts 5:29.)
5. What are the factors which determine how children turn out? What attitude should we take towards those whose children have turned to folly?
6. If you are a parent, list four ways in which you can do better in training your children.
7. If you are a child (hmm … who isn't …), list four ways you can better honour your parents.

12 Wisdom for leaders

The book of Proverbs was written primarily by a king (Solomon) to impart wisdom to future rulers. Chapter 31 begins with words of wisdom taught to King Lemuel by his mother. The books of Kings and Chronicles show how the principles of Proverbs are worked out for good and ill in the lives of the kings of Israel and Judah.

A manual for leadership

Now that there is no longer a theocracy under the New Covenant, how do these principles of leadership apply to us today? The essential teachings of Proverbs about the duties of rulers apply to all nations. Earthly rulers are still to reflect the righteous character of God and are accountable to him. Furthermore, in democratic societies we have the privilege of participating in choosing our leaders and making laws. The principles of Proverbs should be applied by us as we exercise our political rights, seeking to choose leaders who will act wisely and make good laws. Also, the principles about leadership in Proverbs apply to others who are in authority—in the church, in a business, and in the family.

A wise leader reflects God's holy character

Politicians of every political stripe often invoke the name of God in their speeches. On whose side is God? Or better still: Which rulers are on God's side?

He is righteous

Some people claim that it doesn't matter how a ruler lives so long as he or she governs well. But wisdom proclaims that character counts when it comes to leadership: 'It is an abomination for kings to commit wicked acts, for a throne is established on righteousness' (16:12). If a politician wants to have a positive impact on the nation, he or she must live well. If a father wants his children to be righteous, he must set a godly example. Most of the qualifications for leadership in the church deal with moral character, which is more important than charisma or giftedness (1 Tim. 3:1–7).

He is not greedy

'The king gives stability to the land by justice, but a man who takes bribes overthrows it' (29:4). Those in power are often in a position to enrich themselves. There are extensive warnings in the Old Testament against this vice (Deut. 17:16–17; 1 Sam. 8:10–18). One of the qualifications for a leader in the church is that he be 'free from the love of money' (1 Tim. 3:3*b*). The early church was polluted by some leaders who tried to use their positions for financial gain (1 Tim. 6:5; 2 Cor. 2:17).

He is not enslaved to substance abuse

'It is not for kings, O Lemuel, it is not for kings to drink wine, or for rulers to desire strong drink, for they will drink and forget what is decreed, and pervert the rights of all the afflicted' (31:4–5). Substance abuse impairs judgement and makes a leader unfit to carry on his or her responsibilities. The wise man is sober, alert, and self-controlled. Inebriation often leads to other sins, such as fighting, sexual immorality, and blasphemy (20:1). Those who abuse substances suffer physically and financially.

> Who has woe? Who has sorrow?
> Who has contentions? Who has complaining?
> Who has wounds without cause?
> Who has redness of eyes?
> Those who linger long over wine,
> Those who go to taste mixed wine.
> Do not look upon the wine when it is red,
> When it sparkles in the cup,
> When it goes down smoothly;
> At the last it bites like a serpent
> And stings like a viper.
> Your eyes will see strange things
> And your mind will utter perverse things.
> The heavy drinker and the glutton will come to poverty
> (23:29–33,21).

King Belshazzar lost his throne on the night he held a drunken party (Dan. 5). It is required that church leaders are not addicted to wine (1 Tim. 3:3) or other intoxicating substances.

He does not give his strength to strange women

'Do not give your strength to women, or your ways to that which destroys kings' (31:3). The law warned that the king must not 'multiply wives for himself, or else his heart will turn away' (Deut. 17:17*a*). Solomon's heart was led astray by his foreign wives (1 Kings 11). Sexual sin undermines a ruler's moral authority (2 Sam. 12). In the same way, a church leader must be faithful to his wife (1 Tim. 3:2*b*).

He has personal integrity

'Excellent speech is not fitting for a fool; much less are lying lips to a prince' (17:7). A kingdom is founded upon truth and faithfulness to God's moral law. 'Loyalty and truth preserve the king, and he upholds his throne by righteousness' (20:28). When we vote for our leaders, we should ask ourselves, 'Do these people keep their promises?' One way to test this commitment to truth is to see how faithfully such men or women have kept the vows of marriage. Rulers of the church, likewise, must be above reproach (1 Tim. 3:2*a*).

He fears God

'The fear of the LORD is the beginning of knowledge' (1:7). A wise ruler recognizes that God sovereignly appoints and brings down rulers (Dan. 2:21). Such rulers acknowledge that they are under God's authority. They do not become proud or set themselves up as saviours but look to God for security (21:31). When the nation enjoys victory in war or economic prosperity, the wise king does not take credit but realizes he is but a channel of God's blessings to his people (21:1). Because he fears God, he doesn't fear men (29:25) and isn't afraid to alienate the powerful in the cause of righteousness. Pilate is an example of a weak ruler who compromised justice because of the fear of men. Likewise, leaders in the church are to recall that the Lord owns the flock (Acts 20:28*b*). They are not to lord it over those allotted to their charge but are to prove to be godly examples (1 Peter 5:3).

He earnestly seeks wisdom

Wisdom declares, 'By me kings reign, and rulers decree justice' (8:15). The kings of Israel were required to write out a copy of God's law (Deut. 17:18). While our nations are not under the Mosaic Law, God's Word still provides the basis for righteous human government. Without revealed moral absolutes, nations plunge into anarchy. 'Where there is no vision, the people are unrestrained, but happy is he who keeps the law' (29:18). The 'vision' spoken of here is not that from the politician's platform but rather revelation from God. The Bible teaches the rule of God through the law of God. Even the king is subject to the law (see 1 Kings 21). A wise ruler doesn't 'shoot from the hip' but takes the time to fully understand the issues of the day: 'the glory of kings is to search out a matter' (Prov. 25:2*b*; see also 18:17). Such rulers surround

The Bible teaches the rule of God through the law of God.

themselves with wise and righteous advisors (11:14; 16:13) and purge their cabinets of the wicked and self-serving (29:12). Rehoboam lost most of his kingdom when he listened to wicked counsellors (1 Kings 12). We as citizens advise our rulers when we vote or contact our elected officials. The church also is dependent upon infallible and authoritative revelation from God. Many churches and denominations are ignoring God's revelation and governing themselves according to the arbitrary whims of men. Without the authoritative revelation of Scripture, the people of God perish (Prov. 29:18). Within the church, the leaders are to be experts in God's Word and able to teach and counsel others and to refute those who are in error (Titus 1:9). Wise church leaders thoroughly investigate major decisions and seek wise counsel.

He governs justly

'The exercise of justice is joy for the righteous, but is terror to the workers of iniquity' (21:15). While private individuals are not allowed to take revenge on those who wrong them, leaders act on God's behalf when they punish the guilty (Rom. 13:4; 1 Peter 2:14) and are accountable to him for faithfully carrying out this task. 'He who justifies the wicked and he who condemns the righteous, both of them alike are an abomination to the LORD' (Prov. 17:15). Good rulers are passionately committed to righteousness and do not let the guilty go free. 'A king who sits on the throne of justice disperses all evil with his eyes ... A wise king winnows the wicked, and drives the threshing wheel over them' (20:8,26). Such a king is concerned for the rights of the victims of crime. He does not give preference to the rich and powerful: 'If a king judges the poor with truth, his throne will be established forever' (29:14). Nor does such a king rob the rich to gain the votes of the poor: 'Nor shall you be partial to a poor man in his dispute' (Exod. 23:3). He opposes moral evils, which in our day would include the killing of unborn babies and the promotion of homosexuality. 'He who says to the wicked, "You are righteous," peoples will curse him, nations will abhor him' (Prov. 24:24). In the same way, church leaders are responsible for maintaining righteousness in the church. They are to exercise discipline among the members of the church (1 Cor. 5). They may be called upon to serve as impartial mediators in disputes among believers (as in 1 Cor. 6).

Church leaders are responsible for maintaining righteousness in the church.

He protects the rights of the righteous and shows compassion to the helpless

Wise rulers respect the property rights of their people: 'Do not move the ancient boundary or go into the fields of the fatherless, for their Redeemer is strong; He will plead their case against you' (23:10–11). They honour productive citizens (22:29; see also 1 Peter 2:14). They guard the rights of the poor and exploited: 'Do not rob the poor because he is poor, or crush the afflicted at the gate; for the LORD will plead their case' (22:22–23); 'the righteous is concerned for the rights of the poor, the wicked does not understand such concern' (29:7). They protect those who cannot protect themselves: 'Open your mouth for the mute, for the rights of all the unfortunate. Open your mouth, judge righteously, and defend the rights of the afflicted and needy' (31:8–9). These verses have often been quoted in the pro-life (anti-abortion) movement because the unborn are the most helpless among us. In the context, we see that leaders have a particular responsibility to defend the afflicted and oppressed. In the past, leaders such as William Wilberforce spoke out for the afflicted by fighting to abolish the slave trade. Church leaders also have a significant responsibility to care for those in want. A major part of their ministry in the early church was benevolence towards widows and those suffering from famine (Acts 6; 2 Cor. 8–9; Gal. 2:10; James 1:27).

Leaders have an impact on the people

In 1 and 2 Kings, the fortunes of Israel and Judah rise and fall according to the quality of their rulers. 'Righteousness exalts a nation, but sin is a disgrace to any people' (14:34). A good ruler is a channel of blessing from God: the people enjoy prosperity (29:2*a*) and the nation enjoys security. 'The king gives stability to the land by justice' (29:4*a*). Corrupt leaders are a curse: 'When a wicked man rules, people groan' (29:2*b*). We see many examples in the current day of corrupt rulers who exploit and oppress their own people who often become refugees in neighbouring nations. 'Like a roaring lion and a rushing bear is a wicked ruler over a poor people' (28:15). The lack of justice at the top causes evil to spread: 'When the wicked increase, transgression increases' (29:16*a*). God often gives us the rulers we deserve (28:2*a*). Spiritual leaders also have an impact on God's people. When they set a godly example, people follow (1 Peter 5:3*b*). When they are immoral, the leaven of corruption spreads (1 Cor. 5:6). The New Testament makes provision for the removal of unqualified leaders for the sake of the purity of the church (1 Tim. 5:19–20; Acts 20:28–31).

Act wisely towards those in authority over you

We are to respect and obey those in authority over us: 'My son, fear the LORD and the king' (24:21*a*). 'The terror of a king is like the growling of a lion; he who provokes him to anger forfeits his own life' (20:2). The New Testament reminds us that we are to obey those in governmental authority because God has put them in authority over us (Rom. 13:1–7), with the only exception being when we must obey God rather than man (Acts 5:29). Proverbs encourages us to deal wisely, gently, and discreetly with those in power, as Daniel and Abigail did (Prov. 16:14; 23:1–3; 25:15). Elsewhere, the Bible reminds us to pray for our rulers (1 Tim. 2:1–4; see also Ps. 72). We are also to honour those who are over us in the church so that they will find joy in their labours on our behalf (Heb. 13:17).

Jesus Christ is the ideal king

Everything which Proverbs teaches about the ideal ruler can be said of Christ. His character is perfect in righteousness and wisdom. His administration is just. He successfully implements his agenda because he is in complete control of all things. He will judge with complete righteousness and will establish a perfect and everlasting kingdom (Isa. 9:7; 11:1–5; Dan. 2:44; Rev. 21:1–5). He shows great compassion on all who humbly turn to him. 'Now to the King eternal, immortal, invisible, the only God, be honor and glory forever and ever. Amen' (1 Tim. 1:17).

FOR FURTHER STUDY

1. How are the principles for political leaders applied differently under the Old Covenant compared with under the New Covenant? (See Rom. 13:1–7.)
2. If our nations are not 'Christian', from where can our leaders obtain the moral absolutes by which they are to govern? (See 1 Peter 2:14.)

TO THINK ABOUT AND DISCUSS

1. What is the role of government in helping the poor? (See Prov. 29:7; Dan. 4:27.)
2. Why is it wrong for us to take personal revenge but right for the government to punish evildoers? (See Rom. 12:19; 13:1–4.)
3. Do you pray for your political leaders? How should we pray for them? (See 1 Tim. 2:1–4.)
4. What role should the church have in selecting and influencing political leaders? Are there things individual Christians can and should do that the church should not do?
5. Why does God sometimes allow wicked and incompetent people to rule? (See Jer. 27.)
6. Do you pray for the leaders of your church? How do you pray? (See Eph. 6:18–20.)
7. Think of two things you can do to encourage and support your church leaders.
8. How does Jesus fulfil all of the requirements in Proverbs for an ideal king?

13 The wise woman

(31:1–31)

Every year my local newspaper recognizes ten 'women of merit' in my community. One year I wrote a letter nominating my wife, describing how she has devoted her life to training our children, helping me in my ministry, and serving the Lord in our church and the community through many acts of service and charity. Sadly, the newspaper did not select her, but I believe that if Proverbs 31 had been the basis of their criteria, she would have risen to the top of their list.

Which women are worthy of honour?

The world tends to honour women for one of two reasons. Some are honoured because of their outward beauty and charm. Because such value is placed upon physical appearance, many women spend a lifetime trying to gain and preserve the perfect body and face. Women also receive worldly honour when they go out and beat men at their own game in business, government, or sports.

What kind of woman does God honour?

The biblical ideal for womanhood is completely counter-cultural. While our society is trying to obliterate the distinctions between men and women, Proverbs 31 describes a wife whose life is centred on serving the Lord by being a helper to her husband (Gen. 2:24).

Wisdom in the home

The ideal woman is not found in a convent separated from the world but in a home with a husband, children, and dirty laundry. After having been warned of how the Strange Woman can ruin him (Prov. 7), the young man is shown a portrait of the wise woman who will contribute to his success in life. This is a woman you can bring home to your mother! 'An excellent wife is the crown of her husband, but she who shames him is like rottenness in his bones' (12:4). She is not merely a sex object, a maid, and a cook; rather, she is a woman of virtuous character. She is a capable manager, teacher, and entrepreneur, all while living a home-centred life. This is the

> Matthew Henry describes this chapter as a looking-glass for ladies which they are desired to open and dress themselves by.

ideal to which women are to aspire. Matthew Henry describes this chapter as 'a looking-glass for ladies which they are desired to open and dress themselves by, and if they do so, their adorning will be found to praise and honour and glory at the appearance of Jesus Christ'.[23]

There is more to Proverbs 31 than meets the eye

The description of the excellent wife in 31:10–31 is an acrostic in which each verse begins with a consecutive letter of the twenty-two letters of the Hebrew alphabet. The purpose of this arrangement was to aid memory.

Proverbs 31 also has symbolic significance. In addition to describing the ideal wife, this chapter serves as a climax to the teaching of Proverbs by once again personifying wisdom (as in the first nine chapters). The young man is exhorted to embrace Lady Wisdom (1:20–33; 8:1–36; 9:1–6), who shares the attributes of the virtuous woman. She is more precious than jewels (3:15; 8:11; 31:10), makes you rich (3:14; 8:21; 31:11), feeds you (9:1–5; 31:13–15), teaches what is good (4:3–4; 31:26), and fears the LORD (1:7; 31:30).

Search for a woman of excellence (vv. 1–3,10–12)

While Proverbs 31 is written to a man, it can easily be applied to a woman, to whom it would say, 'Become a woman of excellence.'

Listen to your mother (vv. 1–2)

Proverbs 31 contains words King Lemuel (about whom we know nothing) learned from his mother, presumably as he grew up. While most of Proverbs has been the voice of a father speaking to his son, here we have his mother making her urgent appeal for him to act wisely in one of the most important choices in life (1:8*b*).

The wrong kind of woman will ruin you (v. 3)

Before beginning the magnificent description of the wife of excellence, the king's mother warns him against vices that can destroy him and weaken his kingdom (vv. 3–7). The Strange Woman, like strong drink, will drain your strength. She will seduce you, encouraging you to be unfaithful to your marriage vows (7:21–22). If you marry her, she will be unfaithful to you (2:17; 30:20). She is the opposite of the virtuous wife. Instead of strengthening your house, she will demolish it: 'The wise woman builds her house, but the foolish tears it down with her own hands' (14:1). She will neglect your family (7:11). She will bankrupt you financially (6:31). She will ruin your reputation (6:33). She will distract you from your calling. You will be so busy trying to please her (and she is hard to please!) that you will have little time left for your vocation. You won't be able to trust her to run your home. Your kids will be out of control. You will be constantly fighting domestic fires. She will wear you out! 'A constant dripping on a day of steady rain and a contentious woman are alike; he who would restrain her restrains the wind, and grasps oil with his right hand' (27:15–16; see also 25:24; 21:19). There are many biblical examples of women who have been a detriment to their husbands, including Delilah, Job's wife, Jezebel, Michal, and Solomon's foreign wives.

An excellent wife will contribute to your success (v. 10)

'An excellent wife, who can find? For her worth is far above jewels.' She is a strong woman who will strengthen you. The Hebrew word translated 'excellent' (or 'virtuous') is the same word translated 'strength' in verse 3. This word was also used of valiant warriors. The 'weaker sex' is not weak in every sense. Such a woman is a rare and valuable gift from God (18:22; 19:14). Just as God made Eve from the flesh of Adam, only God can create a woman like this for you. Just as the young man is exhorted to search for wisdom, so he should earnestly search out a woman like this, not settling for less.

She is trustworthy (v. 11*a*)

'The heart of her husband trusts in her.' You can trust her faithfulness to your marriage vows. She is not flirtatious or immodest. When you go out of town, you don't have to worry that she will be with another man (7:19). You can trust her with your reputation. She will bear your name with dignity. She will not gossip or reveal your secrets to others. You can trust her with your money (and your credit cards). She won't spend you into debt. You can trust her oversight of your children and household.

She is an asset (vv. 11*b*–12)

'He will have no lack of gain. She does him good and not evil all the days of her life.' The virtuous woman devotes herself to assisting her husband in every way she can, particularly in the domestic realm. Such a husband is richly blessed. I have seen many a man greatly improved by marriage to the right woman. She consistently does him good 'all the days of her life' (v. 12*b*). She doesn't let difficult circumstances or her 'time of the month' prevent her from doing good. She treats her husband better than he deserves because she does it ultimately for the Lord.

She enhances your standing in the community (v. 23)

'Her husband is known in the gates, when he sits among the elders of the land.' The husband's status is mentioned in this chapter about the excellent wife because he wouldn't be where he is in life without her. Because his home is well run, he is able to put his full energy into pursuing success in his vocation. She also serves as a trusted advisor and confidante, helping him to manage his business or career. The man who aspires to be a leader in the church needs a wife like this. A wise old preacher once told his son, 'Your wife will make you or break you in the ministry.'

An excellent wife will help you in many ways (vv. 13–27)

She is home-centred (v. 27)

Her priority in life is to be a helper to her husband (v. 12; see also Gen. 2:18; Titus 2:4–5). She is content to support and share in her husband's success (vv. 23,11*b*). She ignores the screeching feminists who accuse her of wasting her life and claim that she needs to get out of the home to amount to anything. She emulates the Lord Jesus by having a servant's heart: 'Whoever wishes to become great among you shall be your servant, and whoever wishes to be first among you shall be your slave; just as the Son of Man did not come to be served, but to serve, and to give His life a ransom for many' (Matt. 20:26*b*–28). She doesn't need worldly achievement and accolades for fulfilment in life.

She is diligent (vv. 13–14*a*,17,19,21–22)

She uses her time effectively, rising 'while it is still night' (v. 15*a*), and 'her lamp does not go out at night' (v. 18*b*). She enjoys being busy and 'works with her hands in delight' (v. 13*b*). Counsellors have observed that some homemakers are prone to depression because they have less structure in their lives and can easily waste time. This woman, however, is organized and diligent. She possesses physical strength for her tasks (v. 17). Though she is busy with many other interests, she doesn't cut corners when it comes to feeding her family and is willing to go 'afar' to obtain the best quality and price (v. 14). She also ensures that her family is well clothed (vv. 13,19,21–22).

She brings beauty and quality into her home (vv. 14,21–22)

If you want to know what the world would be like without women, visit a man's apartment and see how he lives, eats, and dresses when ladies aren't around. The excellent wife goes beyond the minimum in dress, food preparation, and home decoration; she cooks meals that are tasty, healthy, and even colour coordinated. She brings a woman's touch as she decorates her home and fills it with interesting sights and smells. She takes care of her outward appearance, including her clothes (v. 22) and her body, so that her husband can find delight in her beauty (5:18–19).

She is a responsible administrator (vv. 11,14–16,21,25,27*a*)

Instead of bankrupting her husband by overspending, the wise woman makes him more prosperous, perhaps earning money in cottage industries (vv. 16,24). She exhibits wisdom by planning ahead for the needs of her family (vv. 21,25*b*; see also 6:6–8; 21:5; 30:25). She doesn't procrastinate. Her household is well run because of her careful management (vv. 15,27). She is sensitive to the unique needs of each of her children and is ready to intervene if one is wandering towards folly. Because she manages the family's resources well, she has time and money left over to help those in need (v. 20). Her husband gladly delegates many important responsibilities to her (v. 11). Husbands show respect to their wives by giving them great freedom in managing the home and not micromanaging them.

She is wise in her speech (v. 26)

She exemplifies all of the characteristics of wise speech taught in Proverbs. She is discreet. She doesn't get her husband into trouble by saying foolish things (18:7; 20:19). Nor does she nag him (27:15). She builds up her husband and others with her kind words (15:4). She teaches her children and grandchildren (1:8; 31:1; Titus 2:3–5).

The excellent wife will be richly rewarded (vv. 28–31)

Her glory is in the home (vv. 28–29)

She has devoted herself to her family. The greatest earthly

blessing she seeks is her children's respect and her husband's praise. These she receives in full: her children bless her; her husband appreciates her worth, envying no man. This passage reminds children and husbands of their duty to offer the encouragement such a woman deserves. Because some husbands fall short, not every godly wife receives this kind of praise. Such a wife can take comfort that her praise is from God.

Her beauty is unfading (v. 30)

The world may measure a woman's worth by outward charm and beauty, but those who are wise look beyond the surface. A flirtatious woman may gather a crowd of suitors, but underneath the charm one may find a rotten character. Likewise, worldly women often have physical beauty while lacking character. 'As a ring of gold in a swine's snout, so is a beautiful woman who lacks discretion' (11:22). Mere outward beauty does not last in spite of make-up, exercise, and surgery. A marriage based merely upon outward beauty will fail because the body wilts over time like cut flowers. But the godly woman's inner beauty grows over time. She is adorned by her good works and wise character. A godly man finds his greatest delight in such beauty.

The godly woman's inner beauty grows over time. She is adorned by her good works and wise character. A godly man finds his greatest delight in such beauty.

The secret of her success is that she fears God (v. 30*b*)

Godly women do not succeed in their own strength. The book of Proverbs ends where it began: 'The fear of the LORD is the beginning of knowledge' (1:7). Because of the Fall, virtue does not come naturally. A woman may be tempted to abandon her role as helper and may desire to dominate her husband (Gen. 3:16*b*). But the woman who turns to God in faith is forgiven her sin and receives a new nature. A common complaint I hear from some women is 'I'd be an excellent wife if he were a better husband.' Yet the wise woman's service to her husband is not based upon his worthiness but Christ's. The virtuous woman does not put her ultimate trust in a man, not even her husband (29:25; see also Jer. 17:5–6). She serves God in her home with the strength that God supplies (Jer. 17:7–8).

God will reward her

Even if the world (or even her family) doesn't put the godly wife on a pedestal, God recognizes her worth.

Conclusion

Ladies: Aspire to be a woman of excellence. Don't make Eve's mistake and let the serpent rob you of joy because of promises of bigger and better things outside God's will. Enlist in God's school of spiritual charm and beauty. Older women should teach these things to younger women (Titus 2:3–5). Younger women should seek mentoring from godly older ladies.

Married men: Encourage your excellent wife.

Acknowledge her to be a gift from God. Show her how you delight in her. Love her as Christ loves you. Do all you can to help her find joy in her role in your home. Make her even more beautiful and spotless for the Lord by washing her with the Word of God (Eph. 5:26).

Single men: Seek a woman of excellence. Many young men are attracted to young ladies primarily because of outward charm and beauty. Heed the call of Wisdom and measure a woman according to her spiritual worth. One man once said, 'If I choose a wife for her beauty, I shall love her no longer than while that continues, but if I love her for her virtue, my happiness will remain entire.' Charming, beautiful women are a dime a dozen and can be found at every beach and mall; a virtuous woman is a rare gift from God (19:14).

Christ is our virtue

Some women dislike hearing sermons on Proverbs 31; they walk away feeling guilty because they don't measure up. It is certainly true that all of us fall short of the standards of wisdom set forth in Proverbs. The gospel, however, brings hope. Our perfection is in Christ, who has atoned for our sins and failures and has given his very own virtue to us so that we can stand before God unashamed (Heb. 10:14). God accepts you not based upon how good a wife (or husband) you may have been. Rather, the LORD receives you because he is satisfied with the perfect virtue of Christ which has been imputed to all who trust him.

FOR FURTHER STUDY

1. How have some wives been a detriment to their husbands? (See Gen. 3; Judg. 16; 1 Kings 11; 21; Job 2:9–10.)
2. Give examples of some virtuous women in Scripture. (See Ruth 4; 1 Cor. 16:19; Acts 9:36.)

TO THINK ABOUT AND DISCUSS

1. The role of women has changed dramatically in Western culture in the past generation. How counter-cultural should Christian women be?
2. How do we reconcile the fine clothes worn by the woman in Proverbs 31:22 with the exhortations in the New Testament for women not to pay too much attention to their outward appearance (see 1 Tim. 2:9–10; 1 Peter 3:3–4)?
3. How do we reconcile the outside business activity of the Proverbs 31 woman with the call for women to be 'workers at home' in Titus 2:5?
4. What can a young woman do to prepare herself to be a Proverbs 31 woman?
5. How can an older woman teach the principles of Proverbs 31 to younger women?
6. How, in specific practical ways, can younger women be mentored by older women in your church?
7. If you are a married man, when was the last time you encouraged and praised your wife? What can you do to increase her fulfilment and joy in your family?

Additional resources

Charles Bridges, *Proverbs* (London: Banner of Truth, 1983).

John Crotts, *Craftsmen: Skillfully Leading Your Family for Christ* (Shepherd Press, 2005).

Derek Kidner, *Proverbs: An Introduction and Commentary* (London: Inter-Varsity Press, 1964).

Bruce Waltke, *The Book of Proverbs,* 2 vols (Grand Rapids: Eerdmans, 2004).

Bruce Waltke, *Proverbs,* Audio Series at Believers Chapel, Dallas, TX (posted on the Internet as MP3 files at www.believerschapeldallas.org/tapes/bw-2_proverbs/index.htm.

Endnotes

Introduction

1 **Bruce Waltke,** *The Book of Proverbs: Chapters 1–15* (Grand Rapids: Eerdmans, 2004), p. 55.

2 **Derek Kidner,** *Proverbs: An Introduction and Commentary* (London: Inter-Varsity Press, 1964), p. 13.

Background and summary

3 **Bruce Waltke,** *Proverbs Audio Series,* from www.believerschapeldallas.org.

4 **Waltke,** *The Book of Proverbs,* p. 36.

Chapter 1

5 **Charles Spurgeon,** *Metropolitan Tabernacle Pulpit,* vol. 17 (Pasadena, TX: Pilgrim Publications, 1971), p. 282.

Chapter 4

6 **Waltke,** *Proverbs Audio Series.*

7 **Abraham Kuyper,** "Sphere Sovereignty", in James D. Bratt (ed.), *Abraham Kuyper: A Centennial Reader* (Grand Rapids, MI: Eerdmans, 1998), p. 488.

8 **Charles Bridges,** *Proverbs* (Edinburgh: Banner of Truth, 1983), p. 24.

9 **Waltke,** *The Book of Proverbs,* p.109.

Chapter 5

10 **Matthew Henry,** *A Commentary on the Whole Bible,* vol. 3 (Iowa Falls, IA: World Bible Publishers, n. d.), p. 830.

11 **Waltke,** *Proverbs Audio Series.*

Chapter 6

12 **Waltke,** *Proverbs Audio Series.*

13 **Waltke,** *The Book of Proverbs,* p. 85.

14 Waltke points out the contrast between wisdom, which was created by God, and Christ, who is the eternal Creator (*The Book of Proverbs,* p. 131).

Chapter 7

15 Originally spoken in his sermon to the Baptist Association meeting in Northampton, England, 30 May 1892.

Chapter 8

16 **Plutarch,** *Life of Cato the Elder* (www.quotationspage.com/quote/24296.html). Also see: http://72.14.253.104/search?q=cache:ZST8Que65AAJ:classics.mit.edu/Plutarch/mar_cato.html+Plutarch+wise+men+profit+more+by+fools&hl=en&ct=clnk&cd=9&gl=us.

17 **Charles Spurgeon,** *Metropolitan Tabernacle Pulpit*, vol. 28 (Pasadena, TX: Pilgrim Publications, 1985), p. 399.

18 From a sermon preached by the Revd Dr Thomas W. Strieter, Class of 1957 (Concordia) at the Lutheran School of Theology, Chicago, on Sunday, 20 May 2007.

Chapter 9

19 **Waltke,** *The Book of Proverbs*, p. 103.

20 **Jeremiah Burroughs,** *The Rare Jewel of Christian Contentment*, http://72.14.253.104/search?q=cache:_J1OnU8xbIMJ:housechurch.org/spirituality/burroughs_jewell.html.

Chapter 10

21 **William Shakespeare,** *The Complete Works of William Shakespeare* (Chicago: HA Sumner and Company, 1882), p. 866.

Chapter 11

22 **Bridges,** *Proverbs*, p. 406.

Chapter 13

23 **Henry,** *Commentary on the Whole Bible*, vol. 3, p. 977.

About Day One:

Day One's threefold commitment:

- To be faithful to the Bible, God's inerrant, infallible Word;
- To be relevant to our modern generation;
- To be excellent in our publication standards.

I continue to be thankful for the publications of Day One. They are biblical; they have sound theology; and they are relative to the issues at hand. The material is condensed and manageable while, at the same time, being complete—a challenging balance to find. We are happy in our ministry to make use of these excellent publications.

JOHN MACARTHUR, PASTOR-TEACHER, GRACE COMMUNITY CHURCH, CALIFORNIA

It a great encouragement to see Day One making such excellent progress. Their publications are always biblical, accessible and attractively produced, with no compromise on quality. Long may their progress continue and increase!

JOHN BLANCHARD, AUTHOR, EVANGELIST AND APOLOGIST

Visit our website for more information and to request a free catalogue of our books.

www.dayone.co.uk

Opening up series

Title	Author	ISBN
Opening up 1 Corinthians	Derek Prime	978–1–84625–004–0
Opening up 1 Thessalonians	Tim Shenton	978–1–84625–031–6
Opening up 1 Timothy	Simon J Robinson	978–1–903087–69–5
Opening up 2 & 3 John	Terence Peter Crosby	978–1–84625–023–1
Opening up 2 Peter	Clive Anderson	978–1–84625–077–4
Opening up 2 Thessalonians (in preparation)	Ian McNaughton	978–1–84625–117–7
Opening up 2 Timothy	Peter Williams	978–1–84625–065–1
Opening up Amos	Michael Bentley	978–1–84625–041–5
Opening up Colossians & Philemon	Ian McNaughton	978–1–84625–016–3
Opening up Ecclesiastes	Jim Winter	978–1–903087–86–2
Opening up Exodus	Iain D Campbell	978–1–84625–029–3
Opening up Ezekiel's visions	Peter Jeffery	978–1–903087–66–4
Opening up Ezra	Peter Williams	978–1–84625–022–4
Opening up Hebrews	Philip Hacking	978–1–84625–042–2
Opening up Jonah	Paul Mackrell	978–1–84625–080–4

Opening up Joshua (in preparation)	Roger Ellsworth	978–1–84625–118–4
Opening up Judges	Simon J Robinson	978–1–84625–043–9
Opening up Luke's Gospel	Gavin Childress	978–1–84625–030–9
Opening up Malachi	Roger Ellsworth	978–1–84625–033–0
Opening up Matthew (in preparation)	Iain D Campbell	978–1–84625–116–0
Opening up Nahum	Clive Anderson	978–1–903087–74–9
Opening up Philippians	Roger Ellsworth	978–1–903087–64–0
Opening up Proverbs	Jim Newheiser	978–1–84625–110–8
Opening up Psalms	Roger Ellsworth	978–1–84625–005–7
Opening up Ruth	Jonathan Prime	978–1–84625–067–5
Opening up Titus	David Campbell	978–1–84625–079–8
Opening up Zephaniah (in preparation)	Michael Bentley	978–1–84625–111–5